SAILING TO THE SUN

SAILING TO THE SUN

— CRUISING HISTORY AND EVOLUTION —

WILLIAM H. MILLER

FONTHILL

To the informative, enlightening and always entertaining and enriching cruise ship lecturers.

Front cover image, above: The *Andes*. (*Norman Knebel collection*)
Front cover image, below: Onboard the *Guglielmo Marconi*. (*Tim Noble collection*)

Fonthill Media Language Policy

Fonthill Media publishes in the international English language market. One language edition is published worldwide. As there are minor differences in spelling and presentation, especially with regard to American English and British English, a policy is necessary to define which form of English to use. The Fonthill Policy is to use the form of English native to the author. William H. Miller was born and educated in United States; therefore American English has been adopted in this publication.

Fonthill Media Limited
Fonthill Media LLC
www.fonthillmedia.com
office@fonthillmedia.com

First published in the United Kingdom and the United States of America 2019

British Library Cataloguing in Publication Data:
A catalogue record for this book is available from the British Library

ISBN 978-1-78155-703-7

Typeset in 11pt on 13pt Minion Pro
Printed and bound in England

FOREWORD

I love cruising—it is the best vacation of all. I have been on eighty-five cruises, beginning in the 1960s with a week-long trip from New York to Nassau and back on a wonderful ship called the *Oceanic*. The service, but especially the food, was magnificent. I was hooked. Lots of trips followed: other ships, other lines, other itineraries and ports of call. By the 1990s, when I retired, I took the plunge—the ultimate plunge. I spent ninety-five days and went around-the-world on the great *QE2*. That trip was indeed a dream come true—and we seemed to go everywhere with thirty or forty ports of call. These days, at the age of eighty-four, I am still cruising. I like and enjoy the ships themselves—a hotel that floats, but also your home away from home. I also enjoy the food, service, the attentive care, and I especially like the guest speakers—you learn while you travel. Bill Miller is one of the very best: he brings the history of ocean liners, crossings, and cruises alive.

Yes, cruising is wonderful, and I am happy and proud to write this foreword for Bill's latest book.

John Abbott
New York City
Fall 2017

Bon voyage! There is nothing like a cruise! (*Author's collection*)

ACKNOWLEDGMENTS

Like operating a cruise ship, it takes many hands—"passengers and crew"—to create a book. I am very appreciative to all, and any omissions by me are deeply regretted. First of all, my great thanks to Fonthill Media, to Alan Sutton, Jay Slater, and the fine Fonthill team. Special thanks also to John Abbott for his Foreword and to Anthony La Forgia for great support and generosity.

Further thanks must go to the late Frank Andrews, Captain Bob Ellingham, Dr. Mark and Jay Epstein, Ron Evans, Mr. and Mrs. Charles Fowler, Howard Franklin, Mr. and Mrs. Jerome Katchman, the late Andy Kilk, Des Kirkpatrick, Norman Knebel, Anton Logvinenko, Mark Merchant, Dr. James Merrill, the late Vincent Messina, the late Beatrice Muller, the late Robert Pelletier, and the late Don Stoltenberg.

Companies and organizations that have assisted and deserve mention include Canadian Pacific Steamships, Carnival Cruise Lines, Crystal Cruises, Cunard Line, Delta Queen Steamboat Co., Disney Cruise Lines, French Line, Grace Line, Hamburg-America Line, Hapag-Lloyd, Holland-America Line, Meyer Werft, Norwegian America Line, P&O, Port of Miami Authority, Port Authority of New York & New Jersey, Port of Port Everglades Authority, Port of San Juan Authority, Princess Cruises, Radisson Cruises, Royal Caribbean Cruise Lines, Royal Viking Line, Sea Goddess Cruises, Silversea Cruises, Star Cruises, Sun Line, Viking Ocean Cruises, Wartsila Shipyard, and Windstar Cruises.

CONTENTS

INTRODUCTION

Happily, I have been lecturing—sailing as a "guest speaker"—on cruise ships for some forty years. It all began on P&O's original *Oriana*, and now includes a list of trips on some hundred or so ships and hundreds of voyages (the Caribbean, Europe, South America, Africa, Antarctica, China, etc.). How fortunate for me!

One of my most popular talks is about the history and evolution of the cruise business. Today, that business is booming: more liners carrying more passengers than ever before in all maritime history. The biggest passenger ships yet (such as the 6,600-bed *Harmony of the Seas*) and some of the most luxurious, creature-comfortable ever (such as the gold-plated *Silver Whisper*).

One of the great perks of giving talks on modern-day cruise ships is meeting fellow passengers. Some share tales and reflections of earlier cruises, often on long-gone ships, but also meeting former crew members (officers, stewards, waiters, etc.). Their shared stories add so much to the lives and times of these ships.

In 2017, I went on six cruises as a speaker, touching ports from Panama to Montreal, from Los Angeles to Mykonos. There were more adventures, more lectures, and more passengers met, and hopefully more anecdotes and tales to tell.

Bill Miller
Secaucus, New Jersey
Fall 2017

1

EARLY CRUISING FOR SELECT TRAVELERS

"After dinner, I stretched out on a deck chair. It suddenly came to me that there was nothing, absolutely nothing, that I had to do. No more rehearsals, no first nights, no more leading ladies to cajole. A self-conscious peace descended upon me as I lay there looking up at the stars." That is what Noel Coward wrote in his shipboard diary when he was on a globe-circling, 100-day cruise around the world back in the 1930s. Is there any doubt that Noel Coward—that debonair and discerning world traveler—knew how to live? I think not. Noel Coward loved to live in the lap of luxury, therefore he loved luxury cruising.

A "luxury liner" is most easily defined as a big or major passenger ship. Certainly the terms conjures up an image, often romanticized, of a stately moving object of size and speed, mightily "ripping" through the seas and, in times long past, capped by as many as three or even four smokestacks. Beginning in the late nineteenth century, these great ships—"the floating palaces" as they were often called—moved gracefully across the oceans and between the continents. Their purpose was to move passengers from one point on the globe to another.

Yet there was another type of luxury liner: the luxury cruise ship. These vessels were sent not on line voyages, but on pleasure cruises, carrying passengers who were more interested in the delights of a sea voyage than traveling to a specific destination. These voyages were not simply destination oriented. Instead, ports of call were diversions—simply additions to the schedule of daily activities.

Today, cruising is almost the complete mainstay of the luxury liner business. Even the *Queen Mary 2*, which still offers transatlantic crossings, is run more like a cruise ship than one of those traditional, class-divided steamers of the past. Today, it is mostly aircraft that move travelers from point "A" to point "B."

The very first cruise was said to have been offered to the public in 1858. It was a sightseeing voyage of sorts to the antiquities of the then rather remote Mediterranean. A British ship, the *Ceylon*, owned by the illustriously historic Peninsular & Oriental Steam Navigation Company, known as the P&O, was employed for this voyage. But it was all rather primitive, long before air-conditioned staterooms, lido decks with oval-shaped swimming pools, top-deck zip lines, robotic bartenders, and even the luxury of comfortable tour buses on shore to ferry passengers to all those temples and treasures. Indeed, the *Ceylon*'s passengers were adventurers, filled with the spirit of exploring, and certainly well-heeled.

Earlier, in 1815, an advertisement was run in an Edinburgh newspaper calling for "tourists" and proposing a "cruise" to the remote Faeroe Islands north of Scotland and onwards as far as even more remote Iceland. It was actually far too adventurous for most people of the time, and so the voyage never quite set off.

Following the *Ceylon*'s inaugural pleasure jaunt, cruises remained rather intermittent. They were daring journeys, still restricted primarily to adventurous souls or, as one advertisement called them, "the educational and scientific oriented travelers." However, by the twilight of the Victorian Age, in the 1890s, there were increasing numbers of adventurers who had both the spare time and the funds to make these "voyages of recreation and rest." Germany's Hamburg-America Line, already one of the world's mightiest ship owners, was interested in pursuing this cruising market and so dispatched one of its smaller ships to the West Indies, the Mediterranean, Scandinavia, and, on occasion, to such exotic destinations as Egypt, West Africa, and even Spitzbergen above the Arctic Circle. Quaintly, the eastern Mediterranean was still referred to as the "Orient." In Britain, the well-known Orient Line, which normally ran passenger ships on line voyages to Australia, had also begun to offer leisure cruises to the Mediterranean and, in summertime, to Scandinavia.

Right: Cruising in 1895. (*Hamburg-America Line*)

Below: The first cruise was said to be on P&O's *Ceylon*. (*P&O*)

Above left: Great Scenery: Cruising to the fjords in the late nineteenth century. (*Hamburg-America Line*)

Above right: Off to exotic Egypt in 1900. (*Author's collection*)

Right: An Afternoon at Sea: Sailing to the Mediterranean. (*Hamburg-America Line*)

2

LUXURY GONE TO SEA: THE FIRST CRUISE SHIPS

After World War I, in the early '20s, the cruising concept was picked-up again but at an even greater pace. Cruises now were lengthier, and more expensive. Cruising still had a select following, a very specific clientele: the rich and the retired, and sometimes the famous. Now, even the world's largest liners, such as Cunard's speedy *Mauretania* and the splendid, 46,000-ton *Aquitania*, sought employment away from winter's cold, dreary, and often-ferocious North Atlantic run. There were fewer transoceanic passengers about, and so it was dubbed the "off season." So, these big liners were temporarily made into all-first class floating resort hotels and sent off on Caribbean and Mediterranean itineraries. The palatial *Mauretania* might travel for six weeks to the Mediterranean, calling at such ports as Madeira, Naples, and Villefranche on the famed French Riviera. Passengers traveled in the absolute lap of sea-going luxury, 200 or so millionaires being looked after by 800 or so crewmembers, and newer, increasingly more luxurious ships followed in their wake—ships such as the fabulous *Île de France*, embodiment of what would become *le style paquebot* or "the steamship style." Completed in 1927, she was listed as 43,000 gross tons. She was a ship of Aubusson carpets and Lalique lamps, lavish lounges, a premier restaurant likened to a Greek temple, and a chapel so ornate that it had no less than fourteen pillars. In fact, the *Île*, as she was affectionately called, was the first liner to introduce Art Deco on the high seas. She was a grand and imposing vessel of white pianos and glossily polished black floors, and was described years later as being "early Ginger Rogers." Her staff was prized, hand-picked, and envied—from suave captains to those red-suited bellboys in their tilted pillbox caps and uniforms boasting more than three dozen brass buttons. As on all French Line ships, her kitchens were unsurpassable. French Line public relations boasted proudly that "more seagulls follow the *Île de France* than any other liner because the scraps are better!" She even had a distinctive ambience, coined as "the cheeriest way to cross the Atlantic."

Above left: Some of the world's biggest and grandest liners went cruising beginning in the 1920s. (*Author's collection*)

Above right: Grandeur at Sea: Cruise ship decor in the '20s. (*Author's collection*)

Right: The lavish, Roman-style swimming pool aboard the *Majestic*. (*Norman Knebel collection*)

Above: White Star Line's *Homeric* moored off Villefranche. (*Norman Knebel collection*)

Below: Cunard offered the very first world cruise in 1922. (*Author's collection*)

Right: Shipboard decor imitated shore-side styles. (*Author's collection*)

Above left: Some decor leaned to the exotic: Spanish, Turkish, Moorish, even Egyptian. (*Author's collection*)

Above right: Without air-conditioning, the Winter Garden was a welcome refuge, especially in warm, tropic waters. (*Author's collection*)

Right: By the '20s, most cabins were without private bathroom facilities. Instead, passengers used public facilities and also relied on metal scoops affixed to portholes, which also brought in cooling sea breezes. (*Author's collection*)

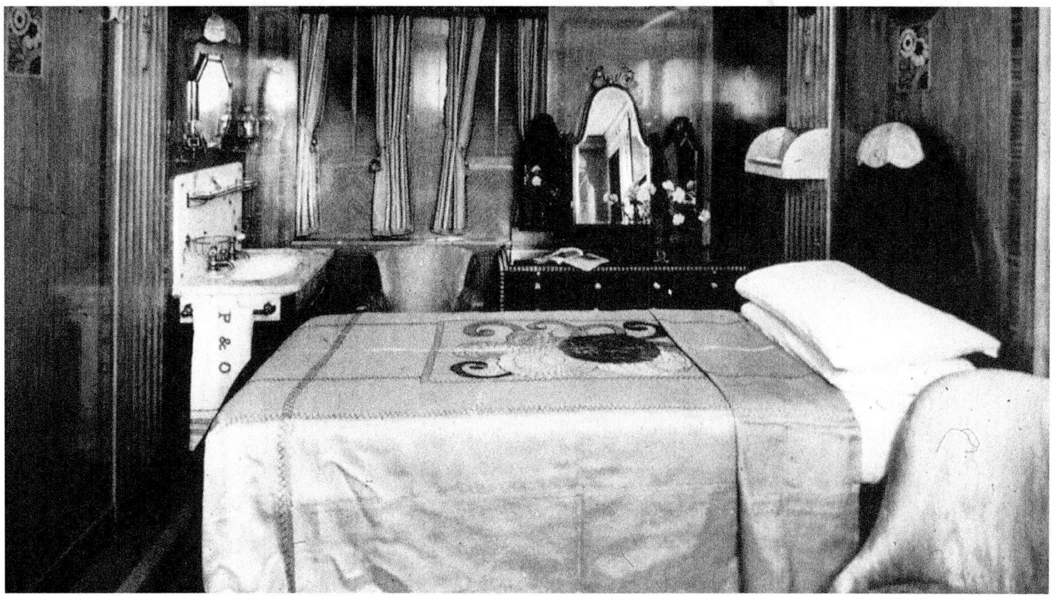

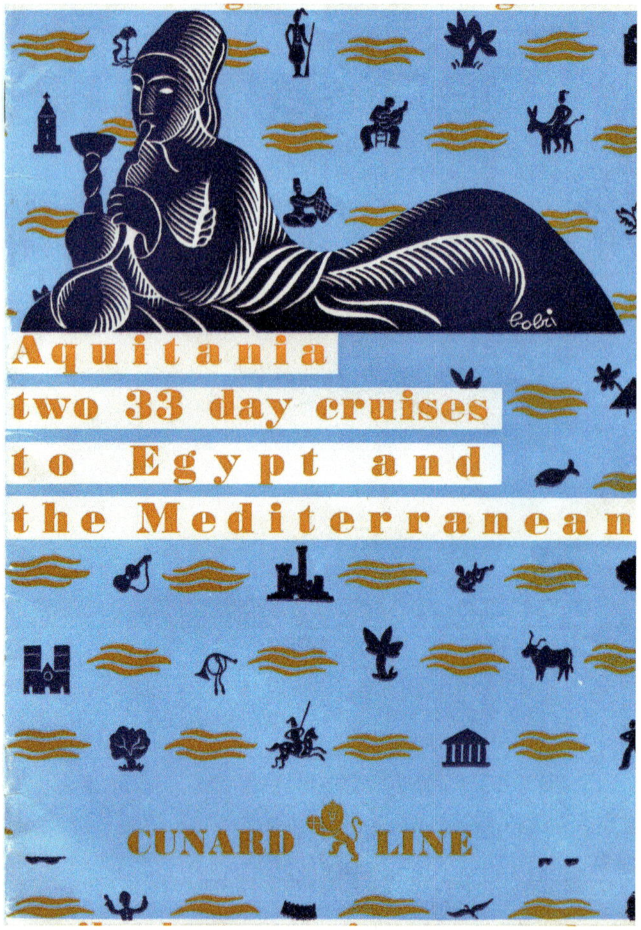

Above left: A Grand Voyage: A six-week cruise from New York to the Mediterranean on the famed *Mauretania.* (*Norman Knebel collection*)

Above middle: Thirty-three days on the magnificent *Aquitania*. (*Norman Knebel collection*)

Above right: Exotic, eye-catching artwork was often used for brochure covers. (*Norman Knebel collection)*

Above left: There were no fitted swimming pools until the 1930s. Instead, passengers sometimes found relief and relaxation in specially erected canvas tanks filled with sea water. (*Author's collection*)

Above right: Tea dances onboard the *Mauretania.* (*Author's collection*)

Right: Sometimes crew members, including the stewardesses, offered evening entertainment. (*Cunard Line*)

3

WORLD CRUISING: THE BEGINNING

To this day, world cruises remain perhaps the ultimate cruise experience. They are lavishly run, splendidly served, and offer an unequal view of the world—from quaint harbors in the Mediterranean to pinhead islands in the Indian Ocean, from glamorous Rio to picturesque Cape Town to the teeming cities of China. Historically, the Cunard Line is said to have operated the first, all-luxury cruise around-the-world (earlier "world cruises" were partly overland by train and therefore not entirely by sea). Cunard's 20,000-ton *Laconia* left New York in November 1922 (three other world cruises left that winter). The roaring '20s had just begun to roar and 300 millionaires set off, mostly with bulging steamer trunks and some with personal servants in tow. The cruise lasted twenty-two weeks. H. L. Mencken, the frequently caustic journalist-author from Baltimore, was aboard one of these early world cruises and noted uncharacteristically for him: "The pure pleasure of it was unimaginable. For days on end, we took to our pews in the Smoke Room, lazily moving from one romantic place to another."

By the late 1920s and into the early '30s, world cruising became an established social ritual for many of the wealthy. There were annual sailings aboard such prestigious liners as Red Star Line's *Belgenland*, Hamburg-America's *Reliance*, and two more Cunarders, the *Carinthia* and *Franconia*. These latter-named beauties developed a loyal following and numbered among their clientele not only members of the world's millionaire elitists, but such celebrated travelers as Noel Coward, Cole Porter, Richard Rogers, Oscar Hammerstein, Mary Pickford, and Douglas Fairbanks. A number of popular songs and even Broadway musicals were first created aboard these ships. For example, Cole Porter and Moss Hart worked on their 1935 musical comedy *Jubilee* during a 34,000-mile world cruise on the *Franconia*. As that 20,000-ton ship headed toward the Fiji Islands, Porter sat down before the upright piano specially installed in his stateroom and tried out a new song for his collaborator. Its title: "Begin the Beguine."

The *Franconia* usually sailed from New York just after the Christmas–New Year holiday—often at midnight—and returned in late May or early June. In a 1931 magazine advertisement, the ship's next winter world cruise was temptingly publicized: "Faraway, glamorous places have stirred your imagination! Bali, still in its primitive civilization; Macassar, flaming like a ruby on the jungle's edge; Bangkok's regal splendor; and Saigon, remote and so special. The *Franconia* includes them without extra cost … and such unique spots as Athens and the Holy Land … and all the other highlights of a round-the-world voyage. One-hundred-and-forty days, 33 ports of call and all at greatly reduced rates, beginning at $1,750."

In the '30s, perhaps no world cruise was as luxurious as those of Canadian Pacific's *Empress of Britain*, a 42,000-ton dreamboat so well appointed it even had her own tennis courts on the top deck. For these long voyages, her capacity was reduced to 750 (down from 1,195) to provide a cozier, more club-like atmosphere to her extraordinary interiors. Her 30,000-mile, 128-day globe-circling runs followed a prescribed annual pattern: eastward through the Mediterranean and Suez to India, Java, Bali, China, Japan, Hawaii, the American West Coast, and finally back to New York via Panama.

In her day, the 758-foot-long *Empress of Britain* was the largest ship to the transit the Suez and Panama Canals. Minimum fares in 1935 started at $2,100 and a suite could cost $16,000. Personal servants went for $1,750 extra.

Above left: The garden-like Winter Garden on the *Franconia.* (*Norman Knebel collection*)

Above right: Cunard's *Carinthia* was one of the great world cruise ships of the 1930s. (*Author's collection*)

Above left: Getting ashore, especially in exotic ports, often took some effort. (*Author's collection*)

Above middle: Glamorous Nights: Cruising on the *Aquitania,* 1933. (*Norman Knebel collection*)

Above right: Exotic Evenings: Cunard's *Laconia* anchored off Istanbul. (*Author's collection*)

Above: The beautiful and mighty *Empress of Britain* at Melbourne in 1939. (*Anton Logvinenko*)

Right: Artists creating steamship posters often made the ships larger than reality. (*Author's collection*)

4

FLOATING COUNTRY CLUBS: YACHT-LIKE CRUISING

By the 1920s, there had been much said and written about the world's great private yachts, certainly those owned by European royals, but also of those owned by flamboyant American millionaires. Although the big liners certainly had a devoted following, the absolute ultimate in travel was a deluxe cruise in a smaller, more intimate ship—a commercial yacht if you will. Norway's Bergen Line was rather clever to recognize this and so—apart from its normal steamer services across the North Sea between Bergen and Newcastle, and along the fabled Norwegian coastline—it saw bright days ahead in the future of luxury cruising. It commissioned a new ship that was deliberately and clearly styled after a sumptuous yacht. She was aptly named *Stella Polaris*, "star of the north." The 5,200-ton vessel was fitted with a very high standard of accommodations. She could never be anything but first class. Some 165 crew members looked after an equal number of guests. There were four special deluxe suites, more than half the other cabins had private bathroom facilities and as many as a third of her cabins were for single occupancy. Her interiors were done in polished woods and a small swimming pool was placed aft. Overall, the ship clearly resembled a yacht. The *Stella Polaris* had an ornate, scrolled clipper bow, twin masts, and a yellow-gold funnel. She appeared beautiful, graceful, and serene. Boarding at Malta in 1930, English novelist Evelyn Waugh wrote for *Harper's Bazaar*: "The *Stella* came from Norway and brought a cold buffet of Baltic delicacies, which is the best I ever encountered."

Above left: The exquisite, yacht-like *Stella Polaris* anchored in Norway's imposing Geirangerfjord. (*Author's collection*)

Above right: At the end of her career, beginning in the late 1960s, the *Stella Polaris* became a floating "country club, restaurant and hotel" in Japan. (*Hisashi Noma collection*)

5

SHORT ESCAPES: "BOOZE CRUISES"

In the same age as the smaller, luxurious *Stella Polaris* and those glorious world cruises on larger liners, such as the *Franconia* and *Empress of Britain*, cruising actually expanded and caught the attention of the general public. In the '30s, in the otherwise hard-pressed, Depression era, ocean voyages became escapes for many, if only temporarily. There were short runs to Bermuda, Nassau, and Havana, and even northern trips up to Halifax, Nova Scotia. Cheapest of all were the overnight "cruises to nowhere," parties at sea with all bars open, despite the rigors of Prohibition. Dubbed "booze cruises," these short jaunts were priced from $10 and often scheduled on such illustrious Atlantic liners as the *Mauretania*, *Berengaria*, and *Majestic*. However, some thought that these liners were demoded. The *Berengaria* was dubbed "the Bargain-area." From these so-called "booze cruises," thousands began to "graduate," if you will, to longer cruises: four, five, and seven days, and then as much as two weeks.

A Christmas cruise to Bermuda cost $43 by 1939, and then there was the *Manhattan* for six days to Havana from $75. Eleven days to the Caribbean in the *Champlain* cost $140 and fifteen days on the *Kungsholm* started at $182. Longer cruises were still popular and, in a three-month period from December 1938, there were fifteen cruises departing from New York of twenty-four days and longer. There were South American trips, all of which put into Rio for its high-spirited Carnival. One of these was aboard the greatest dreamboat ever, France's magnificent *Normandie*.

The 83,000-ton French beauty had her normal 2,000-passenger transatlantic capacity more than halved for her four-week special cruise to southern waters, and that included stops at such ports as Nassau, Martinique, and Trinidad. Her interiors were a public relations agent's dream. The main dining room was done in hammered glass and bronze and with Lalique "towers of light." The gorgeous room was slightly longer than the Hall of Mirrors at Versailles. It rose three decks in height and seated over 700 guests. Caged birds were part of the Winter Garden. The theater was the first ever installed in a liner and the indoor pool was 80 feet of tiled, graduated water levels. The main lounge was done in Dupas panels and Aubusson tapestries, and each first-class suite and stateroom featured a different decor. Aboard one of the first *Normandie* voyages in 1935, British author Harold Nicholson wrote to his wife, Vita Sackville-West: "The whole ship gives one exactly but exactly, the impression of an *exposition des art decoratifs*. It is just like the very best hotel one can conceive."

Above left: Tropic Days: The glorious *Mauretania* was repainted in cooler white in 1933 and used for mostly short cruises. (*Author's collection*)

Above right: Morning Fun: Deck games in 1930. (*Cunard Line*)

Right: Relaxing at Sea: Days with little, even nothing to do. (*Author's collection*)

Above left: During the Depression years, cruising was seen as an escape from worries and financial pressures at home. (*Author's collection*)

Above middle: Cunard-White Star cruise brochure, 1934. (*Norman Knebel collection*)

Above right: Cruising to the cool, scenic Far North on Hamburg-America Line, 1935. (*Author's collection*)

Left: Three Days to Halifax: Deck games on the mighty *Berengaria*. (*Cunard Line*)

Above left: Short Getaways: Cruising to Bermuda, Nassau, Havana, and Nova Scotia on Italian Line's *Roma.* (*Author's collection*)

Above middle: Sweden's *Kungsholm* was a very popular cruise ship in the '30s, and for long as well as short cruises. (*Author's collection*)

Above right: The magnificent *Normandie*—said to be the most luxurious liner then afloat—made two cruises from New York to Rio in 1938 and 1939. (*Author's collection*)

6

THE HONEYMOON SHIP: *QUEEN OF BERMUDA*

Bermuda became very popular and the ideal cruise destination by the early '30s. Consequently, Britain's Furness-Bermuda Line built two small-scale, Atlantic-style liners especially for weekly six-day New York–Bermuda cruises. Carrying over 700 all-first-class passengers each, the *Monarch of B*ermuda and *Queen of Bermuda* quickly became two of the most successful cruise ships on all the seas. Because of their convenient Saturday afternoon departures and fares from $55, the *Queen of Bermuda*, like her sister, became known as the "honeymoon ship." The *Queen* continued after World War II, until 1966, and remained very popular.

Ron Evans worked for several British passenger ships in the early 1950s. "It was a great life for those times. Britain was still caught up in austerity and rationing, and by traveling overseas we could buy food and bring it home," he recalled:

> I'd worked on P&O liners, but my favorite was the Furness-Bermuda Line. And my favorite ship was the *Ocean Monarch*, which was like a big yacht and carried only little more than 400 passengers. Mostly, she was on the 40-hour run between New York and Bermuda. Charlie Chuckles was the captain of the ship and it was said he knew every sandbank around Bermuda. The ship made mostly 6-day cruises and was often filled with single American women. We'd have an overnight on Fridays at Pier 95 in New York and the Market Diner was the place where all the guys used to meet. In those days, we were always dressed when we went ashore—always in suits and ties.
>
> Later, I served on the *Queen of Bermuda*, also on the six-day run out of New York. Working on those Furness ships, I was considered a "first class waiter" and later I found work ashore—in the best hotels in New York City and Miami Beach.

Dr. Mark and Joy Epstein became cruise loyalists—over fifty cruises on one luxury line plus another fifty or so with other companies. "Our first cruise was our honeymoon—May 1950," they told me. "We were young, poor, but excited. We were down on Z Deck in a cabin that was a shoebox -- well, smaller than that. Two bunk beds & barely enough room to stand. The steward, much older and very British, treated us like children during the first week of school. He was our guide for everything. The ship was the *Queen of Bermuda*, it was 6 days altogether and the fare was $250 for both of us. Today, a ship like the *Queen of Bermuda* would be a tub. But then, on our honeymoon, it was a wonderful beginning."

Above left: 600 Miles Away: In the '30s, Bermuda became a very popular cruise destination from New York. (*Author's collection*)

Above middle: Artist Don Stoltenberg's evocative painting of the *Queen of Bermuda*. (*Don Stoltenberg collection*)

Above right: Baggage was marked with well-done identification. (*Author's collection*)

Right: The *Queen of Bermuda* departs from Hamilton, Bermuda, heading home to New York. (*Author's collection*)

7

BRITISH CRUISING: *ARANDORA STAR* AND *ATLANTIS*

Cruising—leisure voyages to "new and exciting places, and often following the sun"—grew steadily in popularity in the 1920s. By the '30s, cruises were offered for as little as a pound-a-day (or $5) and departed from the likes of London, Liverpool, and Southampton. Especially popular were winter runs to the Mediterranean, Madeira, and Canary Islands. These offered escapes, if only temporarily, from the dark, dreary British winters.

Royal Mail Lines found cruising to be interesting, to be an alternative service and to be profitable. They began promoting these voyages that "escaped the everyday routine." While the Company had offered some cruising in the pre-World War I years, it was in 1923 that it all became more serious and purposeful. Their "new" *Arcadian* was introduced to fulltime cruising.

Carrying 350 passengers in all-first class configuration, the *Arcadian* cruised from Southampton to the Mediterranean, West Africa, the Atlantic Isles, to the Norwegian fjords and Baltic cities in summer, and occasionally between New York and Bermuda. She was an instant success, drawing returning passengers and pleasing Company accountants. In 1925, her fleet mates, *Orbita*, *Orca*, and *Ohio*, were running occasional cruises as well. The *Orca* tended to cruise between New York and the Caribbean, while the *Ohio* was chartered for voyages to the Mediterranean, especially to Rome for Holy Year pilgrimages. Meanwhile, the *Orca* made the occasional long, luxurious cruise, such as "The Three Continents" cruise in the winter of 1926. In sixty-five nights, she cruised from Southampton to the Caribbean, then along the East Coast of South America and then over to South and East Africa.

As the U.K.–South American liner trades slumped somewhat, Royal Mail actually saw better returns in cruising. In 1927, both the *Avon* and *Araguaya* spent considerable time cruising rather than on line voyages. However, by 1929–30, the Company opted to concentrate their cruise operation in an even more specially outfitted ship, the 15,600-grt *Atlantis*. She would become one of Britain's most popular cruise ships in the years between the wars. Her first cruise was in the summer of 1930.

She too had been reconditioned, having been the 1913-built *Andes* and used on the three-class, South American liner trade. Sensibly renamed *Atlantis*, repainted in all white, and with all-first-class accommodations for a rather club-like 450 passengers, she was a very purposeful, very well-fitted ship. She had many single cabins, for example, and each fitted with beds (rather than bunks), electric fans, and hot and cold running water. There was a single sitting in the dining room, two verandah cafes, and the novelty of an American bar featuring a new craze: mixed cocktails. There was also a gymnasium, portable swimming pool, lots of open-air deck space, a hair salon, as well as barber shop, gift shop, excursion office, and well-equipped hospital. Activities included evening dancing on deck (and under the stars), deck games, sunbathing, evening cinema, nightly entertainment, and occasional special events: Welcome Aboard Dinner, Carnival Night, Masquerade Ball, Parade of Hats, and Pirates Night. Food and service were of very high levels and sometimes appraised as being even greater than first class on the *Asturias* and *Alcantara* on the South American liner run. Happily, by the late '30s, Royal Mail could boast of more than 50 percent returning customers on some *Atlantis* cruises. Her voyages were described as "cruising at its best," and yet, in competition with the likes of Blue Star Line's renowned *Arandora Star* and Cunard's splendid *Carinthia* and *Franconia*. The *Atlantis* was also noted as being very steady—"a very good sea boat," commented one of her captains.

A sample cruise program from Southampton for the *Atlantis* in 1935 read:

Feb.	Canary Islands, West Africa, Portugal (20 days)
Mar.	Mediterranean (23 days)
Apr.	Mediterranean (23 days)
May	Western Mediterranean (19 days)
Jun.	North Africa & Portugal (15 days)
Jul.	Northern Capitals (13 days)
Jul.	Norwegian fjords (7 days)
Aug.	Northern Capitals (15 days)
Sep.	Mediterranean (21 days)
Sep.	Mediterranean (18 days)
Oct.	Mediterranean (17 days)
Dec.	Canary Islands, Madeira & West Africa (20 days)

From its London offices, Royal Mail would send out "cruise post cards" to passengers, reminding them of forthcoming voyages. Fares were reasonable: seven nights to Norway was available from 11 guineas or approximately 12 pounds ($10) in 2017 currency.

Occasionally, the *Atlantis* would also make longer, more luxurious cruises—such as to the West Indies, South America, the Pacific and Indian Oceans, and to ports in the U.S.A. Business grew such that both the larger *Asturias* and *Alcantar*a would take breaks from their three-class South American sailings and offer cruises. In January 1935, for example, the *Asturias* set off from Southampton on a sixty-five-day cruise through the Mediterranean and Suez, then to Ceylon, the Straits Settlements, the East Indies, and then home via South and West Africa. Fares began at 145 guineas.

Another British shipping company, the Blue Star Line, saw a bright future in 1930s cruising. Their *Arandora Star*, used on the London–South America service, was converted to the luxury cruise ship for a clubby 354 passengers. She did long, varied itineraries, including a cruise to South Africa, another to Rio, and one from England to the Caribbean, which also included a call to the small, rather remote harbor of Miami (today, the biggest and busiest cruise port in the world).

Cruising from British ports (as well as elsewhere in Europe) grew increasingly popular, probably because it offered a quick, inexpensive escape from the daily grind, and prices were right for the times: £6 (or approximately $18) for six days to Madeira on the *Mauretania*; £8 for seven days to Gibraltar and Tangier on the *Aquitania*; and £13 for fourteen days on the *Viceroy of India*, sailing north to Oslo, Copenhagen, Stockholm, and Leningrad. Comparatively, manual workers earned £5 for a fifty- to fifty-three-hour workweek in the 1930s.

Artist Kenneth Shoesmith was a great master of 1930s steamship art. (*Author's collection*)

Above: Kenneth Shoesmith's busy scene of the *Atlantis* moored off Dakar in West Africa. (*Author's collection*)

Below: The gloriously tropical *Arandora Star.* (*Author's collection*)

Left: Off to the historic Mediterranean on Royal Mail Lines' *Atlantis*. (*Norman Knebel collection*)

Above left: Off to the Orient, including Shanghai, on Canadian Pacific's Empress liners. (*Author's collection*)

Above middle: To the Northlands on Cunard's splendid *Carinthia* in 1936. (*Norman Knebel collection*)

Above right: Cruising to Three Continents: South America, Africa, and Europe. (*Norman Knebel collection*)

Above left: Southern Seas: Sailing to Rio and Buenos Aires on Hamburg-South America Line. (*Author's collection*)

Above middle: Norway's beautiful fjords were very popular cruise destinations. (*Author's collection*)

Above right: More Exotically: A cruise to remote Spitzbergen on Hamburg-America Line. (*Author's collection*)

8

CRUISING GERMAN STYLE: "STRENGTH THROUGH JOY"

"Kraft durch Freude" (KdF: "Strength Through Joy") was the section of the Third Reich's national labor organization Deutsche Arbeitsfront (DAF: German Labor Front). It organized leisure activities on an increasingly larger scale for German workers and their families, offering, among other things, inexpensive cruising holidays. This program was started by the Nazis in 1934, using passenger ships that had been hard-hit by the Depression and might otherwise have been laid-up. It included such liners as the *Stuttgart*, *Berlin*, *Der Deutsche*, and *Monte Rosa*. The Nazi-inspired concept was single-class cruising, open to all passengers without any form of class distinction or shipboard separation. Many of the passengers on KdF cruises in the late '30s were in fact country people unused to the rituals even of domestic travel. One farmer is said to have been told to place his shoes outside his cabin door for polishing, but when the steward attempted to carry them off, the farmer slapped him!

The success and popularity of these cruises led to the creation of two specially designed liners, in fact the world's first large all-cruise passenger ships. The 25,500-ton *Wilhelm Gustloff* (named for an assassinated Nazi official) came first and was commissioned in the spring of 1938. Owned by the DAF, she was managed by the Hamburg–South America Line (today known more widely as container ship giant Hamburg–Sud). Launched by Adolf Hitler himself, she later made worldwide news as a floating polling station on 10 April 1938, the day of the plebiscite that ratified the Nazi takeover of Austria. On that day, she sailed to Tilbury (London), took aboard 2,500 German and Austrian residents of Britain, who voted on Hitler's plebiscite once the ship left territorial waters, and later returned them to port. The 684-foot-long *Wilhelm Gustloff* could carry as many as 1,465 passengers.

German maritime historian Hans Georg Praeger wrote:

> [The *Gustloff*] became the pacesetter for construction of special cruising ships. All passengers had outside cabins, thanks to a new type of cabin arrangement. A larger, four-bedded inner cabin surrounded a smaller two-bed outer cabin and was connected by a light passage with the outer wall and the porthole. Incidentally, the *Gustloff* was the world's first sea-going ship on which, according to instructions, the crew had to be accommodated in exactly the same manner as the passengers. The KdF insisted on ample deck space for deck chairs and sports and games as well as large, bright halls with seating accommodation for every holidaymaker and without having to use the dining halls for this purpose. The *Gustloff* and her near-sister, the *Robert Ley*, also had sophisticated fire-safety systems as well as large searchlights, which were fitted to the foremasts and mostly used to light the coastline at night for the enjoyment of the passengers.

Slightly larger (at 27,300 tons), the *Robert Ley* followed in the spring of 1939. It has been said that as many as eight additional, big Nazi cruise ships were planned, but that idea never materialized owing to the beginning of war in September 1939. The *Robert Ley* was managed by the Hamburg-America Line for the DAF. Both ships were purely passenger carriers, meant for leisurely voyages, and so were comparatively slow, making only 15½ knots at best.

Both ships were victims of World War II, destroyed in the final days of that conflict in early 1945. The *Gustloff* was torpedoed and capsized in the bitterly cold, icy Baltic while evacuating Germans from Nazi-occupied Poland. Her loss, on 30 January 1945, ranks as the worst maritime tragedy in history: some 5,200 refugees, prisoners, wounded soldiers, and crew members were lost. The actual figure, vague because of the lack of official records or passenger lists, may be as high as 5,400 or even 6,000. This horrific event has been the subject of several books, mostly German, and films, but was not brought to the full attention of Americans until a television documentary was shown in 1998. The *Robert Ley* was bombed two months later, during the Allied air raids on Hamburg in March 1945. Her scorched, twisted remains were scrapped after the war.

Above left: Exercising and fitness were emphasized on KdF cruises in the late '30s. (*Author's collection)*

Above right: Strength Through Joy: The big Nazi cruise ships *Wilhelm Gustloff* and *Robert Ley*. (*Author's collection*)

Above: The *Robert Ley* prepares for her maiden cruise. (*Author's collection*)

Below: Two KdF cruise ships at Hamburg—the *Oceana* (left) and *Wilhelm Gustloff* (right). (*Author's collection*)

Right: It might be Marlene Dietrich—German cruising in the '30s. (*Author's collection*)

9

HIGH LUXURY: CUNARD'S *CARONIA*

The first big liner built specifically for full-time cruising appeared just after World War II. She was Cunard's renowned *Caronia* of 1948. She became the pacesetter of 1950s cruising. A 34,000-tonner that often carried as few as 300 passengers (her actual cruise capacity was 600) on her long-distance travels, she had the overall feel of a floating country club. Onboard standards were impeccable, the lifestyle elegant, and her 600 or so staff members came close to anticipating the needs and requests of guests. She was the preferred ship among Cunard's entire sea-going staff. Dubbed "the Green Goddess" because of her unique coloring, the *Caronia* went around-the-world almost every winter (otherwise, she did a grand tour of the entire Pacific), and then, in spring, summer, and fall, she cruised the Mediterranean and Scandinavia.

Aboard the 715-foot-long ship there were tales of passengers, women especially, who lived aboard for months, and sometimes years at a time. One still holds the all-time record when she stayed for fourteen years! Some guests never went ashore, more than a few played bridge every day of their cruise, and many had chauffeur-driven limousines meet them in every port. One passenger chartered an entire railway coach during a shore excursion in India, another gave a party for 300 fellow passengers at Hong Kong's Repulse Bay Hotel, and still others flew-in personal physicians and nurses.

Stories abound from the legendary *Caronia* cruises. One woman left the ship in Australia for a week, flew to London for tea with the Queen Mother, and then rejoined the ship three or four ports later. A gentleman had his favorite Champagne flown in from his own vineyards in France. Cunard obliged by stocking favorite wines, breakfast cereals, and even special brands of ice cream. Some women even booked an extra cabin just for their clothes. One *Caronia* world cruise regular always traveled with at least 300 dresses for ninety-five days and nights.

Sailing day on the *Caronia* was like a "big reunion," recalled a couple of *Caronia* regulars:

> There were so many repeaters and everyone knew one another from years and years of travel together. Once underway, these passengers threw great theme parties and invited hundreds of fellow passengers. They paid for all the drinks, but the ship provided other refreshments. Being invited to some of these gala events made for the most wonderful memories.

The service was "absolutely magnificent," those *Caronia* regulars recalled. "Anything you wanted you could have. Your clothes were always laid out and your shoes always polished. Of course, we dressed every night except Sundays. The restaurants—there were two—were *à la carte*. Special dinner requests could be made at lunch and they were prepared."

Right: The beautiful, all-green *Caronia*. (*Author's collection*)

Below left: The bedroom of a top suite onboard the *Caronia*. (*Author's collection*)

Below right: The lavishly spacious sitting room of the same suite. (*Author's collection*)

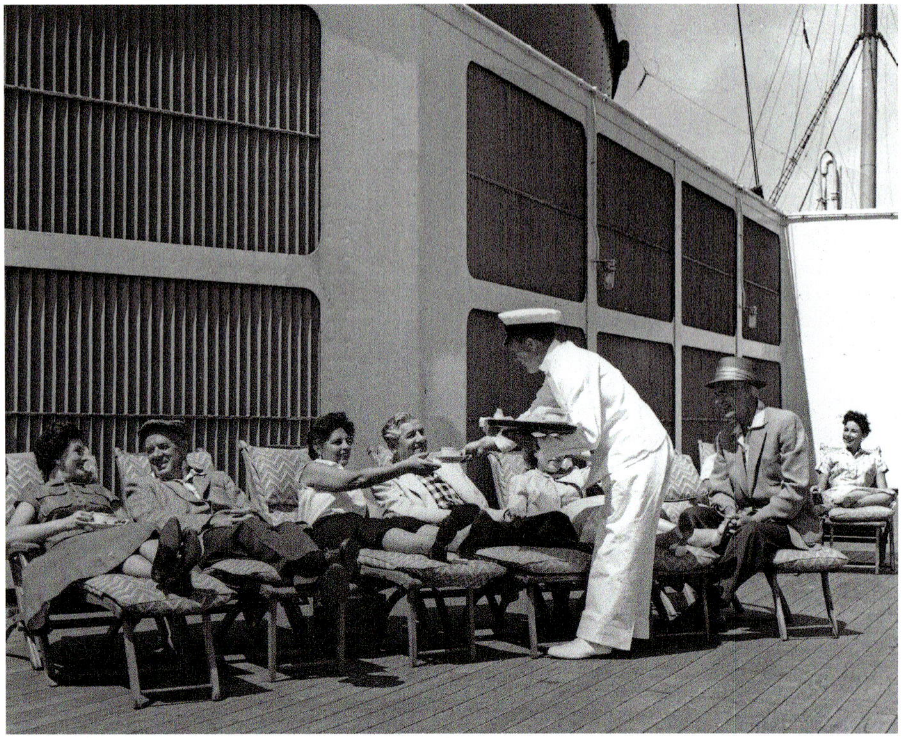

Above: On Deck: Aboard Cunard in the '50s. (*Cunard Line*)

Below: Cunard was, for many years, at the very top of the ocean liner business. (*Author's collection*)

Right: Another legendary world cruise on the *Caronia*. (*Andy Kilk collection*)

10

EVOLUTION: CRUISING IN THE '50S AND '60S

In the '50s and '60s, cruising was primarily a winter business—voyages of escape from the cold, snow-filled Northeast in the U.S., for example—but increased in popularity and gradually evolved to year-round sailings. From New York, there were the likes of the *Queen of Bermuda* and *Nassau* offering weekly runs to Bermuda and Nassau; and on longer, more port-filled voyages to the Caribbean on ships such as the sisters *Santa Rosa* and *Santa Paula*, and the *Victoria*. Cruising from Florida was in its infancy and called only for aged, converted steamers such as the *Evangeline*, *Yarmouth*, *Bahama Star*, and *Florida*. A three-day weekend cruise from Miami to Nassau and back was priced from $59 in 1959. But the good life remained. Aboard the illustrious Hawaiian cruise ship *Lurline*, a cruise director recalled:

> There was tremendous elegance aboard ships like Matson Line's *Lurline* and her sister ship *Matsonia*. There was dressing for dinner—and the passengers wanted it that way. Midnight buffets were served by chefs in enormous white hats, carving a baron of beef, and surrounded by magnificent set-ups of sculptured ice.

A loyalist to another great ship, the *Nieuw Amsterdam*, noted: "The service was of another age. It was strict French silver service. There were trays of meats and others for vegetables."

By the 1960s, the lengthy, luxury cruise market was overtaken by newer ships: Sweden's *Gripsholm* and *Kungsholm*, Norway's *Bergensfjord* and *Sagafjord*, and the Dutch *Rotterdam*. Des Kirkpatrick was a cruise staff member on Holland America's most lavish of voyages: the annual ninety-five or so day cruise around the world. These grand trips, the ultimate circumnavigations in ways, began sailing in January 1961. Sensibly, the Company used the exquisite *Rotterdam*, then brand new, but thoughtfully gave her a more clubby tone by specially reducing her total capacity of 1,456, in two classes, to a more intimate 700, completely first class, of course. Kirkpatrick recalled: "These were gala, very special trips. There were ladies who traveled with a million dollars just in jewels and others who sailed with 200 and 300 dresses for 90 days. They would have so-called 'day clothes,' morning attire and then dresses just for late afternoon, for very formal teas, and then, of course, lavish gowns for evenings."

Above left: Sixty winter days away on the *Britannic*'s Mediterranean cruise in 1956. (*Andy Kilk collection*)

Above right: The glories of cruising in the sunny Caribbean. (*Grace Line*)

Right: Grand Evening: Dining on Cunard, 1960. (*Cunard Line*)

Above left: Deck games on the *Mauretania*. (*Cunard Line*)

Above right: Repainted in shades of green, the stately *Mauretania* looked more tropical for cruising. (*Author's collection*)

Right: Cruising to the top of Norway—onboard the *Vistafjord*. (*Norwegian America Line*)

South to the West Indies on Home Lines' hugely popular *Homeric*. (*Author's collection*)

Above: Cruising from Britain: The splendid *Andes*. (*Author's collection*)

Below: Leisurely Days: Grace Line's *Santa Rosa* arrives off Cartagena as part of a twelve-night cruise from New York. (*Author's collection*)

Left: From two weeks to the Caribbean to six weeks completely around South America on Swedish–American Line's *Gripsholm*. (*Author's collection*)

Right: Caribbean cruises from Port Everglades on the German *Hanseatic*. (*Author's collection*)

Below left: Cruising on the impeccably fed and served *Île de France*. (*French Line*)

Below middle: Cruising to the Eastern Mediterranean: Greece, Turkey, and Egypt. (*Author's collection*)

Below right: Winter cruising to the sun-drenched Caribbean on the luxurious *France*. (*French Line*)

Above: Five Days: From San Francisco to Honolulu aboard Matson Line's *Matsonia*. (*Author's collection*)

Right: Thirty-eight days, sixteen ports, and fifteen countries—cruising to the Mediterranean on Cunard's *Mauretania*. (*Norman Knebel collection*)

11

SLEEK ITALIAN DECOR: THE INNOVATIVE *OCEANIC*

At lunchtime on a sunny April day in 1965, New York harbor was noisier than usual: a new liner was arriving in port for the first time. Tugs created a welcoming escort, fireboats sprayed, and helicopters buzzed overhead. The ship, all white, with a flair bow and a funnel placed aft and resembling, say, an oil tanker, she caused a stir, something of a sensation. She was the 39,000-ton *Oceanic*, owned by the multi-national, but immensely popular Home Lines. She flew the Panamanian colors, however, a flag of convenience that avoided taxation as well as the likes of crew unionization and regulations. New York dockers, among others, were somewhat resentful and dubbed her a "Runaway Flagship." Yet she was a great sensation: glorious interiors in her 774-foot-long hull, twin pools covered by a retractable glass ceiling, and she offered renowned Home Lines' food and service.

The 27-knot, Italian-built *Oceanic* was also a great innovator; in the infancy of year-round cruising, she offered weekly departures (every Saturday afternoon at 4 p.m.) from New York on seven-night cruises to Nassau and back. Minimum fares were $175 and went up to as much as $1,000 for a top-deck suite. In winter, between December and April, she made longer cruises: ten to twenty-one day trips around the Caribbean islands. Booked months and sometimes years in advance, the exquisite *Oceanic* had legions of loyalists. For twenty years, she was a beloved fixture in New York harbor.

Sold to Premier Cruise Lines in 1985, she was marketed as the *Starship Oceanic* for twice-weekly cruises over to the Bahamas from still-budding Port Canaveral. In 2000, she became the *Big Red Boat I*, but soon reverted to *Oceanic*. After Premier collapsed two years later, the 1,136-berth ship passed over to Spain's Pullmanturs, running weekly cruises in and around the western Mediterranean from Barcelona.

Yet time was running out by 2008. Against her forty-three years, she had become less and less economical. For the Spanish, she had become the "honeymoon ship." She would leave Barcelona every Monday, a convenience for Saturday marriages. She carried mostly younger passengers. The average age was thirty-five, but some were as young as eighteen. The Spanish passengers were reported to be fun but often noisy, though never annoying. On many cruises, there were also lots of Spanish-speaking South Americans onboard.

By 2009, the *Oceanic* had gone on to a new, quite different life—as the roving cruise ship for the Japan Peace Boat Society. Her voyages, which were mostly world cruises, even included a visit to familiar waters: New York. One visitor remembered: "The *Oceanic* was still a great ship, but little remained of the original interior décor. But some visitors could still stroll the public rooms and corridors and remember as she was. Some even had old deck plans and brochures in hand."

The *Oceanic* had a career of some forty-seven years. Its final voyage, in July 2012, was to Zhoushan, China, where veteran ship was broken-up for scrap.

Above: The innovative *Oceanic* was commissioned in April 1965. (*Vincent Messina collection*)

Below: The *Oceanic*'s seven-day cruises between New York and Nassau were tremendously popular. (*Author's collection*)

Right: The pool deck on the *Oceanic* was covered by a retractable glass "ceiling." (*Author's collection*)

12

RUNAWAY TO SEA: LONG VOYAGES ON P&O–ORIENT LINES

Beginning in the mid-'50s, two important British passenger ship lines decided to venture up and away from its long-established voyages between England and Australia and include the North American West Coast. Consequently, after leaving Sydney and Melbourne (and sometimes Auckland and Wellington), liners belonging to the P&O and the Orient lines sailed northward to Fiji and Honolulu and then to Vancouver, San Francisco, and Los Angeles. Later, this link to the South Pacific was extended to include the Far East (Yokohama, Kobe, Hong Kong, and Singapore) and sailing to and from Britain via Mexico, Panama, the Caribbean, Port Everglades, Nassau, and Bermuda. Sailings (by the specially dubbed Orient & Pacific Line) became more frequent and were run by a virtual armada of big liners: *Orcades*, *Himalaya*, *Chusan*, *Oronsay*, *Arcadia*, *Iberia*, and *Orsova*. In 1960–61, by then retitled P&O–Orient lines added their biggest, fastest, and most luxurious liners, the 2,134-passenger *Oriana* and the 2,272-passenger *Canberra*.

The long, port-filled P&O–Orient voyages might be—including connections with second and even third ships—as long as 100 days and touch several dozen ports. With the ships being two class (first and tourist), the fares were almost bargain-like for the 1960s: from $18 per person in first class and from $11 in tourist class. One P&O repeater recalled:

> P&O offered a wonderful shipboard experience for me: Lots of curries at meals, deck games, lots of young fellow passengers and charming, hardworking Indian stewards and waiters. And, of course, it was very, very British—the noon whistle, quizzes and afternoon tea. And which was my favorite ship? Well, I must say it was the *Arcadia*. She had this special charm and warmth that few other liners had or ever had.

"The *Arcadia* was my favorite P&O liner of all," said Howard Franklin, a longtime passenger and frequent guest lecturer aboard the great P&O Lines, one of the most illustrious shipping lines and still sailing today but as Carnival Corporation-owned P&O Cruises. In earlier days, up until the 1970s, P&O Lines was mostly interested, however, in long-haul, two-class passenger ship services, usually between Britain and Australia, but also to other parts of the world. Their liners touched on over 100 ports in all.

"P&O-Orient had wonderful ships, but for me, the *Arcadia* had something special about her," remembered Franklin:

> She had the most wonderful library with club chairs. You can just curl-up and read a good book. P&O ships differed from their close rivals, the big liners of the Orient Line, which was also British. P&O was more equalitarian. There was less aristocracy in first class, for example. Orient Line ships felt like big country houses gone to sea while P&O liners were more hotels at sea. Orient Line also had better food and impeccable service in first class and which was superior to P&O.

As a greater age of all-first class cruising on more modern, amenity-filled ships emerged beginning in the 1970s, P&O–Orient abandoned most of its worldwide, two-class liner operations and became P&O Cruises.

Above left: P&O-Orient's well-liked *Arcadia* making a turn off the Sydney Opera House, 1972. (*Frank Andrews collection*)

Above middle: The *Himalaya* was another popular P&O-Orient liner. She sailed until 1974. (*P&O*)

Above right: Around-the-world—a "Seven Seas Adventure"—onboard the *Oronsay* in 1969. (*P&O*)

Left: Sunshine cruising on P&O-Orient in the 1960s. (*P&O*)

Above left: The fine-looking *Chusan* passes under the famed Sydney Harbor Bridge. (*P&O*)

Above right: The *Oriana* berthed at Sydney in July 1984. (*Author's collection*)

Right: To American ports on P&O. (*Author's collection*)

13

INNOVATIVE NEW COMERS: NORWEGIAN CARIBBEAN AND ROYAL CARIBBEAN

In the mid-'60s, Scandinavian ship owners—operating freighters, tankers, and other assorted cargo tonnage—began to see the greatest promise in cruising, and they fine-tuned this interest: they saw great promise in the Florida–Bahamas–Caribbean cruise trade and so formed specialized new firms with the first generations of specially designed and built cruise ships.

Norwegian Caribbean Lines was formed by Norway's Knut Kloster, who partnered with shipping agent Ted Arison (who would later form his own firm, Carnival Cruise Lines, in 1971). NCL's first ship was a small, 8,600-ton cruise ship/car ferry, the *Sunward*. She offered three-night cruises from Miami over to the Bahamas with rates beginning at $59. It was a quick success and led to larger, improved versions: the *Starward* and *Skyward*. NCL was both intuitive and aggressive, and this led to many cruise innovations that have since become standards in the industry. As examples, NCL offered the first out-island experience, the first to develop new ports in the Caribbean, and the first to operate (by 1980) a super liner, the converted *France* that became the *Norway*, for weekly, seven-night Caribbean cruises from Miami.

Norwegian Caribbean, later renamed Norwegian Cruise Lines, eventually expanded to worldwide operations. Between 1997 and 2001, NCL even operated cruises from Australia as the Norwegian Capricorn Lines, and for Hawaiian cruising, NCL America. NCL also acquired other cruise lines: Royal Viking in 1984, Royal Cruise Line in 1990, and Orient Line in 1998. NCL itself was bought by Malaysian–Hong Kong-owned Star Cruises in 2000, but then was partly sold again in 2008 with 50 percent going to a financial investment company, Apollo Management.

Today, Norwegian Cruise Lines is one of the world's biggest and most popular cruise operators, with over a dozen big liners in service and as many as six on order for the future (2018–2022).

Norwegian Caribbean's early success certainly prompted others to look seriously at the Florida–Caribbean cruise market. In 1968, three well-known Norwegian ship-owners—Anders Wilhelmsen & Co., I. M. Skaugen & Co., and Gotaas Larsen—joined together to form Miami-headquartered Royal Caribbean Cruise Lines.

Film queen Ingrid Bergman named the first of three, gleaming-new, 750-passenger sister ships, the *Song of Norway*. Entering service in 1970, she was followed by two sisters, the *Nordic Prince* and *Sun Viking*. Business boomed, and by 1978, both the *Song of Norway* and *Nordic Prince* had to be enlarged, being given 85-foot midsections and increased berths to over 900. Further, continued success was on RCCL's radar screen. The *Song of Norway*—over twice the size of the 18,500-ton *Sun Viking*—was added in 1982. A long list of new, increasingly larger ships followed, resulting in the 228,000-ton, 6,600-passenger *Harmony of the Seas* in 2016.

RCCL (later rebranded as Royal Caribbean International) has long since expanded beyond the Caribbean. By 2017, the Company has twenty-five ships offering worldwide cruise itineraries, and the Company has a near 22 percent of the world cruise market. They have also acquired as well as invested in other cruise lines. Amid their more prominent holdings, they own Celebrity Cruises and Azamara Cruises outright, and they have half ownership of TUI Cruises, Pullmanturs, and CDF Croisieres de France.

Above left: Early Ships: One of Norwegian Caribbean Lines' first cruise ships, the *Starward*, seen at San Juan. (*Author's collection*)

Above right: Initially, some NCL ships were intended to carry cars as well as cruise passengers. (*Author's collection*)

Right middle: Laid-up in 1974, the famed *France* was sold to Norwegian Caribbean Lines in 1979 and then converted to the cruise ship *Norway.* (*Author's collection*)

Below right: The transformation of transatlantic to tropic cruise ship was highly successful—the *Norway* arrives in New York in May 1980. (*Author's collection*)

Above: The *Norway* received an enthusiastic reception at New York on a May morning in 1980. (*Author's collection*)

Below: The *Norway* was the beginning of bigger and bigger cruise ships. (*Author's collection*)

Left: The *Norway* carried two big tenders, named *Little Norway 1* and *Little Norway 2*. (*Norwegian Caribbean Lines*)

Above left: These tenders eased the offloading of some 2,200 passengers in smallish Caribbean ports. (*Author's collection*)

Above right: These tenders were also used to land passengers on NCL's "private island" in the Bahamas. (*Author's collection*)

Right: Contrast: The 18,500-ton *Song of Norway* of 1970 compared to the 76,000-ton *Sovereign of the Seas* of 1987. (*Royal Caribbean International*)

The innovative *Sun Viking* moored at Ocho Rios, Jamaica. (*Author's collection*)

A nightclub high up in the funnel. (*Author's collection*)

Above left: Airport styles goes to sea! The low ceilinged, simplistic decor of 1970 aboard the *Song of Norway* and her sisters. (*Author's collection*)

Above right: Cabins were smaller, partially in effort to get the passengers to come out, participate, and spend money. (*Author's collection*)

Right: In 1978, the seven-year-old *Nordic Prince* was sent back to her builders in Helsinki to have an 85-foot-long midsection inserted. (*Wartsila Shipyard*)

Above: The 550-foot-long ship was immediately cut in half. (*Wartsila Shipyard*)

Above: The 85-foot-long, prefabricated mid-section. (*Wartsila Shipyard*)

Below: The "surgery" was done in a large, covered shed. (*Wartsila Shipyard*)

Below: The project was completed in three months and was done with great precision. (*Wartsila Shipyard*)

Above: Job Complete: The extended *Nordic Prince*. (*Wartsila Shipyard*)

Below: In the '60s, Miami was little more than a "sleepy, backwater port." In this scene, dated 1964, the *Bahama Star* and *Ariadne* are on the left; the *Riviera Prima* and *Florida* in center; and the *Yarmouth* on the far right. (*Author's collection*)

Right: Seven Liners in Port: Miami became the biggest, busiest cruise port. (*Port of Miami Authority*)

Above: Less than 20 miles north, Port Everglades is the second busiest. (*Port of Port Everglades Authority)*

Left: San Juan, Puerto Rico, became increasingly popular for cruising deeper into the southern Caribbean. (*Port of San Juan Authority*)

Above left: Nassau has long been a popular cruise port, especially for short three- and four-day cruises from Florida. (*Author's collection*)

Above right: Nassau and the Eastern Caribbean were voted (in 2015) the most popular cruise destination. Busy Day: Ships in port include the *Starward*, *Carnivale*, *Dolphin*, *Emerald Seas*, *Galileo*, *Sunward II*, and *Starship Oceanic*. (*Author's collection*)

Below left: St. Thomas was voted by cruisers as the most popular port in the Caribbean. (*Author's collection*)

Below right: Trans-Panama Canal cruises, beginning in the '70s, have become increasingly popular. (*Princess Cruises*)

Above: Alaska is the third most popular cruise destination. (*Holland-America Line*)

Below: Glacier Bay offers an extraordinary setting and scenery. (*Holland-America Line*)

Right: Ships are often dwarfed by the mighty Alaskan Glaciers. (*Holland-America Line*)

Above: Cruising to South America: The *Stella Solaris* off Rio de Janeiro. (*Sun Line*)

Above: South Pacific: Cruising from Sydney on the *Oriana*. (*P&O*)

Left: South Pacific cruising has boomed in recent years. (*Norwegian Cruise Lines*)

14

CRUISING EMPIRE: MIGHTY CARNIVAL

Carnival is phenomenal: they are the biggest, most diverse, most popular, and certainly most successful passenger ship owner and operator of all time. By 2017, Carnival Corporation owned ten cruise brands: Carnival Cruise Lines, Holland America, Princess, Seabourn, Cunard, P&O, P&O Australia, Aida, Costa, and, as of 2017, a Carnival China cruise division was in the works. Through these arms, Carnival has a 49 percent share of the entire world cruise market. Miami-headquartered Carnival Cruise Lines itself has twenty-five large cruise liners (2017) and with four additional mega-ships on order. In North America, the world's biggest cruise market, Carnival and its affiliates have a 21 percent share of the cruise market.

Formed by Ted Arison, who had been with Norwegian Caribbean Lines, Carnival was created in 1971. The new Company had very humble beginnings.

Carnival's initial three cruise ships were secondhand acquisitions. The 27,200-grt *Mardi Gras* was the first, added in the winter of 1972. She had been the *Empress of Canada*, built for British-flag Canadian Pacific Steamships in 1961. The second, the *Carnivale*, joined the fleet in 1975. She too had been with Canadian Pacific, having been launched in 1956 as the *Empress of Britain* (and which later became the Greek Line's *Queen Anna Maria*). The third was the new company's largest yet, and the largest in weekly Miami–Caribbean cruise service. It was the 38,000-grt, 1,450-passenger *Festivale*, which started her days as the British-registered *Transvaal Castle* of the Union-Castle Line and, before being sold, sailed also as the *S. A. Vaal* for a Union-Castle partner, the Safmarine Lines (the South African Marine Corporation).

"Carnival Cruise Lines began on a very small, very tight budget," noted the late Robert Pelletier, who began working in the south Florida cruise industry in the early 1970s:

> They opened a Miami office with a small core staff. There were 4 or 5 sales reps whereas today [2002] there are probably 500. The *Mardi Gras* was brought over from London, where she had been laid-up as the *Empress of Canada*, and immediately was placed in service. Cheerfully colored contact paper was placed over the ship's dark wood panels. Workmen were aboard for at least the first six cruises. They would close-off a small portion of the ship, with the passengers aboard, and make alterations. One dining room was actually ripped out during one of the first cruises and rebuilt as cabins before the ship returned to Miami seven days later!

"On the first six cruises, the *Mardi Gras* was transformed—made over as a cruise ship, a glitzy Carnival cruise ship," added Pelletier. "But spending was kept to a minimum. The Canadian Pacific funnel logo, for example, was kept. It was simply repainted in red, white and blue."

Mark Merchant, an amateur ventriloquist, applied to Carnival, and within days, he joined the *Mardi Gras*:

> I thought I was being hired as a cabaret act, but in those days everyone had many "hats" on Carnival ships. I did my own shows as well as sold

> and hosted shore excursions, ran bingo and horse-racing, oversaw deck games, attended the singles' parties and rotated as emcee for the evening show times. The days were very long on Carnival back then. I was paid $250 a week [1975]. But the *Mardi Gras* was a great fun ship, indeed the first of the so-called Carnival "fun ships."

Merchant was later posted to the 25,000-ton *Carnivale*, which was not his favorite ship and one he described as "old and grubby with a grim atmosphere." Next, he went to the *Festivale*, then (1978) just converted in Japan for tropical cruising. "She was then the largest ship in year-round Caribbean service," he noted:

> She also began the guest performer program at Carnival. Now, we were required to have scripts, outlines, a consistency to our acts. Music was added to the presentation and you were introduced by an actual cruise director. A greater bond developed between the cruise staff and the entertainers. But you were still requested to host all sorts of events. There was horse-racing at 8 in the morning, several daily games of bingo and the almost constant selling of rainbow-colored, enticingly named drinks. There were many revenue-producing activities onboard. From a staff point-of-view, you see an aggressiveness in Carnival. There were no doubts—there was growth ahead. NCL and Royal Caribbean were then said to be superior, even better to work aboard, but you just knew that Carnival would one day overtake them. Within ten years of its creation, by 1982, Carnival had their first brand new ship, the *Tropicale*. It is not surprising that today they have the biggest fleet in ocean liner history!

Begun in 1971, Carnival has grown to be the biggest, most expansive passenger ship liner ever. (*Author's collection*)

Above left: Grandmother: The *Mardi Gras*, the former *Empress of Canada*, was the very first Carnival cruise ship. (*Carnival Cruise Lines*)

Above right: Carnival Cruise Lines itself is the leading cruise line in the huge North American market. (*Carnival Cruise Lines*)

Left: The *Fantasy*, arriving at Miami, can carry up to 2,600 passengers. (*Carnival Cruise Lines*)

Above left: Carnival ships are noted for their often glitzy, Las Vegas-style decor. (*Carnival Cruise Lines*)

Above right: The highly successful 70,000-ton *Fantasy* class of ships of the 1990s. (*Carnival Cruise Lines*)

PARADISE

Carnival Destiny

Above left: Entrance lobbies have expanded to eight and ten decks in height. (*Carnival Cruise Lines*)

Above right: In the mid-1970s, the Soviet Union had the largest passenger ship fleet—and included ships often chartered out to Western cruise lines. (*Author's collection*)

Opposite above left: When she was commissioned in 1998, the *Carnival Paradise* was the first totally "smoke free" cruise ship. (*Carnival Cruise Lines*)

Opposite above right: When it was commissioned in late 1996, the *Carnival Destiny*—refitted as the *Carnival Sunshine* in 2013—became the first Carnival ship to exceed 100,000 tons. She ranked, for a time, as the largest liner afloat. (*Carnival Cruise Lines*)

Opposite below left: While the shows hint of Broadway, Las Vegas, and London's West End, the rooms themselves have grown to 2,000 and 3,000 seats. (*Carnival Cruise Lines*)

Opposite below right: Dining sometimes has as many as three sittings for dinner—one being just for families with children. (*Carnival Cruise Lines*)

15

SEA-GOING LUXURY: THE THREE ROYAL VIKING LINE SISTERS

I am often asked, usually aboard current cruise ships, about the whereabouts of some long-ago ships. Sometimes it is the ship from that very first, indelibly remembered cruise. Occasionally, we would go back farther, to the great and grand age of Atlantic liners, ships used on those magically memorable summertime trips to and from Europe. One of the ships, in this case three sister ships, was the Royal Viking Line trio: *Royal Viking Star*, *Royal Viking Sea*, and *Royal Viking Sky*.

"The Royal Viking Line was perhaps the finest company we have ever cruised with," said Mr. and Mrs. Jerome Katchman:

> They were impeccable, the very finest in their time, possibly the best ships ever. Their three original ships—the *Royal Viking Star*, *Sky*, and *Sea*—carried no more than 550 passengers, which was so club-like, friendly, intimate and even cozy, and which altogether meant one sitting for meals in the restaurant. We love one-sitting. There's no rushing, no time restriction, no strict regimentation in the evenings. The food as well as the service on Royal Viking were impeccable. They employed the finest staff—from the officers to the cruise directors to the waiters and stewardesses. Everyone seemed to be handpicked. In fact, many of the officers and hotel staffs and even entertainers of current luxury cruise liners started at Royal Viking. Captain Reidulf Maalen, the first master of the *Crystal Serenity* in 2003, began at Royal Viking. He recalled, "They were an excellent training ground. And, of course, they also had constantly changing itineraries. We loved that. We could stay on two or three cruises and yet not repeat the same ports. And their ships traveled just about everywhere in the world."

Royal Viking, based in Oslo, but with operational headquarters in San Francisco, was created by three Norwegian ship-owners to fill a void in the luxury, high-end cruise market in the early '70s and also to meet the expanding demands of the growing international cruise market, but particularly in the U.S. Their three new ships were the grand successors to the likes of Cunard's impeccable *Caronia*, the renowned, all-green, world-roving cruise ship that carried up to 600 guests per cruise, which were looked after by 600 top staff and crew, but was retired from service in 1967. Royal Viking's prime competitors were such gold-plated ships as the *Kungsholm* and *Gripsholm* of the Swedish American Line (which sadly left the sea-lanes in 1975) and the *Sagafjord* and *Vistafjord* of Norwegian America (then sold to Cunard in 1983). Built by the Wartsila Shipyard at Helsinki, the 21,847-ton *Royal Viking Star* was the first of the new trio, being commissioned in June 1972. Twin sisters, the *Royal Viking Sky* followed in June '73 and the *Royal Viking Sea* that November. They soon established sterling reputations and developed loyal, returning passengers.

Inevitably, the cruise business grew more and more competitive as passenger ship operational costs not only increased, but soared (it was once rumored that Royal Viking Line actually never really earned a profit). Profitability, or at least potential profit, had to be rethought. Greater, increased capacities were seen as a route, especially by eager, often-worried home office accountants. So, in 1982–83, the three 550-foot long ships were sent off to Bremerhaven, West Germany, and where they were "stretched"—being fitted with 120-foot-long midsections, which increased their capacities and supposed profit-making capacities to as many as 812 passengers in all. The ambience, cozy charm, and single sittings were suddenly gone, along with some loyalist, early Royal Viking followers. "Things were never quite the same again," according to the Katchmans.

A larger version of the three original ships, the 37,000-ton *Royal Viking Sun*, was added in 1988 along with a small, yacht-like, but generally misplaced ship, the *Royal Viking Queen*, which carried only some 200 passengers. At about the same time, Royal Viking itself was sold off to other Norwegians, to the Kloster Group, which owned Miami-based Norwegian Cruise Lines. With five ships now in the Royal Viking fleet, there was soon some shuffling and reshuffling of tonnage. Once again, there were changes to the gold-plated, paradise-at-sea world of Royal Viking.

The *Royal Viking Star* was transferred, in a sort of Viking demotion, to the Norwegian Cruise division in 1991 and became the mass-market *Westward* before going over to yet another Kloster arm, Royal Cruise Lines, in 1994 and changing to *Star Odyssey*. She was sold off completely in '96 to the Fred Olsen Line, also Norwegian, but which used England as the base of its cruise operations. The former *Star* currently sails as the *Black Watch*.

The *Sky* began dividing her time in 1991: summers in the Baltic Sea as the *Birka Queen* and then, with a quick coat of paint, for the remainder of the year out of Florida (and to more tropic ports) as the *Sunward*. Unsuccessful, she was chartered within two years (in '93) to Princess Cruises, who sailed her for three years as the *Golden Princess*. In '96, she was swung over to NCL's new parent, Malaysia-based Star Cruises, and began sailing in Asian waters as the *Super Star Capricorn*. Her itineraries, at least in '98, included overnight "dinner & gambling" cruises out of New York. Next stop: later in '98, she was chartered to the South Koreans, Hyundai Merchant Marine Lines, who were anxious to develop a local Far Eastern cruise business. Now, she was the *Hyundai Kumgang*. Less than a success, she went back to Star Cruises in 2001, reverting to *Super Star Capricorn*, but had little work and was then laid-up for over two years. European cruising began to boom by 2004 and so she was chartered to the Spanish, to Iberojet, who sailed her out of Barcelona as the *Grand Latino*. But a year later, she was sold off—going, like the former *Royal Viking Star*, to Fred Olsen, who extensively refurbished and upgraded her as the *Boadicea*, but soon renamed her as the present-day *Boudicca*.

Finally, the original *Royal Viking Sea* was transferred within the Kloster family to Royal Cruise Lines in 1991, changing names to *Royal Odyssey*. Six years later, in '97, she rejoined NCL as the *Norwegian Star*, but for a new, short-lived arm, Norwegian Capricorn Lines, on cruises out of Sydney, Australia. She slipped over to parent Star Cruises by 2001, but she was now sailing in mostly Chinese waters as *Norwegian Star I*. In almost a flash, she was off to the Mediterranean as the renamed *Crown*, now owned by the Dutch, the Cruise Club of the Netherlands, but chartered to the Spanish. However, that ended by 2004, when she was chartered to the Germans, to Phoenix Reisen, based in Bonn, for current worldwide cruising as the 884-passenger *Albatros*.

Royal Viking Line itself eventually withered away. The largely unsuccessful *Royal Viking Queen* was sold off to Seabourn, where she joined her near-sisters, *Seabourn Pride* and *Seabourn Spirit* as the *Seabourn Legend*. The Royal Viking name along with the 754-bed *Royal Viking Sun* was sold off by Kloster to the Cunard Line in 1994. It became Cunard-Royal Viking until the Royal Viking name was dropped altogether (and in the wake of Carnival's purchase of historic Cunard the year before). Afterward, under the Carnival umbrella, the 38,000-ton ship was herself transferred to Seabourn in '99, becoming the *Seabourn Sun*; later, in 2002, she joined another Carnival arm, the Holland America Line, who sail her these days as the *Prinsendam*.

Above left: Royal Viking Line continued, in the '70s, high luxury on the high seas. (*Author's collection*)

Above right: Royal Viking was among the very first to introduce guest speakers during days at sea. (*Royal Viking Line*)

16

THE *PACIFIC PRINCESS*: THE "LOVE BOAT"

She is gone now, reduced to rubble and scattered debris in Aliaga, a remote but busy ship demolition port in Turkey. In the summer of 2013, it was finished with engines for the infamous Love Boat, best remembered as the *Sea Venture*, but more especially as the *Pacific Princess*. She reached the scrapyard, coming from Italy and in the hands of a small skeleton crew, but then almost immediately took a severe list, began to cant over, and all but slammed into another liner waiting for her turn with the shipbreaking crews, another ship with a string of names beginning with *Fairsky* and then *Sky Princess*. However, it is the ex-*Pacific Princess* that has a special—in fact, very special—place in cruising history.

Back in the 1960s, even the seafaring Norwegians could not have predicted the great rate of success of the North American cruise industry. Cruising, especially to the sunny Caribbean, was still rather seasonal, but it was soon to become year-round, including seven-night itineraries from two emerging Florida ports: Miami and Port Everglades. Norwegian Cruise Lines was one of the great forerunners, beginning in 1966 with their brand new if smallish *Sunward*. Royal Caribbean followed in 1970, but other Norwegians were looking to invest. Among these were two well-known cargo and tanker owners, Oivind Lorentzen and Fearnley & Eger. They decided, in 1969, to enter the promising American cruise trades with two 20,000-tonners. More specifically, they saw potential in the weekly run between New York and Bermuda. The two ship owners created a new operational arm, New York-based Flagship Cruises.

Built in West Germany, the two new liners were named *Sea Venture* and *Island Venture*. They had space for 646 all-first-class passengers or 750 maximum berths. Commissioned in May 1971, the *Sea Venture* was used as the Bermuda ship, sailing almost every Saturday at 4 p.m.; the *Island Venture* followed in late 1971, but tended to do seven- to eighteen-day Caribbean cruises. All seemed well, popular, and profitable until, beginning in 1973, fuel oil prices soared. Running passenger ships became more complicated. The Norwegian owners soon began to have second thoughts. Flagship was in trouble, and so, in October 1974, the two liners were sold to Britain's P&O for their American subsidiary, Princess Cruises.

"We built the *Spirit of London* [1972] as our bid to move into cruising, especially North American cruising," recalled P&O Captain Bob Ellingham:

> I was transferred to the Los Angeles offices of Princess Cruises, a company that we bought [in 1974] so as to expand more rapidly. At first, however, we worked as P&O Lines. We developed a rather good following with the *Spirit of London* and intended to acquire two more cruise ships, the Norwegian *Sea Venture* and *Island Venture*, which were to become the *Spirit of Liverpool* and *Spirit of Southampton*. P&O wanted to model their cruise division after the then new Royal Caribbean Lines of Miami. They used the name *Song of Norway* for their first ship and so we used *Spirit of London*. It was a new age for passenger ships and so new identities. Old ways and names were being

> pushed aside to an extent. But then we acquired Princess Cruises from Mr. Stanley McDonald of Seattle and we realized Princess had an even stronger following. Consequently, we adopted the Princess concept—the *Spirit of London* became the *Sun Princess*, the *Island Venture* as the *Island Princess*, and, subsequently best known of all, the *Sea Venture* as *Pacific Princess*. The very popular television series *The Love Boat* was first filmed on the *Sun Princess* [in 1975], but then quickly moved to the *Pacific Princess*. For the next dozen or so years, the *Pacific Princess* was just about a household name. Lots and lots of people wanted to sail in her, hoping the television cast and stars would be aboard. Many volunteered to be "extras" in the filming sequences. That series turned out to be a stroke of genius. It turned Princess Cruises into a major cruise line, but also greatly helped the competition as well.

Historically, Flagship Cruises itself actually made a comeback. First, they planned to charter Holland America's then laid-up *Veendam* and sail her as the *Sea Venture II*, but that plan never materialized. In late 1975, they bought Swedish America Line's impeccable *Kungsholm* and entered the long, luxury cruise market. It was all rather short-lived, however: in 1978, Flagship closed down altogether and the *Kungsholm* was sold, coincidentally, to P&O, becoming the *Sea Princess*.

Based at Los Angeles, the *Pacific Princess* and *Island Princess* became very popular with their seven- to fourteen-day itineraries to the Mexican Riviera, trans-Panama Canal, Caribbean, and, in summer, up to Alaska. Yet greater acclaim and special popularity was ahead for the 550-foot-long *Pacific Princess*.

In the mid-1970s, a television pilot for a possible series was planned about life aboard a cruise ship. There was to be no disasters, no murders, no slapstick comedy, but three themes per hour-long segment built around love and romance. Aptly, the production was called *The Love Boat*. It was soon a weekly series, one lasting eleven years. In a stroke of tremendous good fortune, and with a rapidly assembled cast of familiar characters headed by an affable captain and pretty cruise director, episodes were sometimes filmed aboard, but always said to be on, the *Pacific Princess*. Princess soon capitalized on the relationship by, among other touches, having the show's catchy theme song played onboard, and even if most episodes were filmed in a Hollywood studio, passengers happily waitlisted for those few sailings where television cast and crew would actually be aboard. Soon, *The Love Boat* cruises moved away from Mexico and the Caribbean, and headed to Alaska, the South Pacific, Australia, and Europe. By the mid-1980s, the U.S. cruise business passed the $4 billion annual level. *The Love Boat* was cited as one of the three contributing factors to the extraordinary growth (the others being the ease of air-sea combinations and the appeal of theme cruises). The series was seen by almost 40 million Americans each week, and many were convinced to book their first cruise—hopefully to have fun, maybe find a husband, or perhaps meet the likes of guest stars like Lana Turner on deck! One Princess captain later reported: "Assuredly, *The Love Boat* has been a stroke of genius for us. But it has also served and benefited our competitors as well."

As newer, bigger, and flashier ships were added to the Princess fleet, however, the *Pacific Princess* was sold off in 2002. She became the *Pacific* for Spain's Pullmanturs, alternating between summer Mediterranean and winter South American itineraries. In the end, and after being laid-up at Genoa for almost six years, she was sold to the Turks for scrapping.

Additionally, the ex-*Island Princess* had also been retired. After having sailed for several operators including the South Korea's Hyundai Cruises, she had been operating as the U.K.-based *Discovery* in recent years. However, aged and much less economical, the forty-three-year-old ship headed for demolition in India in 2015.

Above: Beginnings: The little *Princess Patricia* was the first ship for Princess Cruises. (*Canadian Pacific*)

Below: The *Island Princess* (left) and *Sun Princess* meet at Vancouver. (*Author's collection*)

Right: Princess Cruises has evolved to great popularity. (*Princess Cruises*)

Left: The *Pacific Princess* became the "Love Boat," which added greatly to her recognition and popularity. (*Princess Cruises*)

Below left: Princess quickly expanded beyond the Mexican Riviera and cruised, in summer, to Alaska and then to a worldwide scope. (*Princess Cruises*)

Below right: Pacific Tranquility: The *Pacific Princess* in Tahitian waters. (*Princess Cruises*)

17

MEDITERRANEAN FAVORITE: THE *STELLA SOLARIS*

The blue-hulled, Greek-owned *Stella Solaris* was a very popular cruise ship. For nearly thirty years, she was especially well known in the Eastern Mediterranean, mostly for her seven-day cruises from Piraeus to the nearby Greek islands and to Turkey, Israel, and Egypt. Yet she also cruised the Caribbean, made trips around South America, and became one of the earliest cruise ships to sail the exotic, picturesque Amazon River, making the 1,000-mile journey from the Atlantic coast to the interior city of Manaus. I was aboard her for one of these trips, in December 1985. She was also especially well known for her Caribbean cruises out of Galveston, Texas. In the mid-1980s, during a slump period for Mediterranean–Greek isle cruising, especially following the headline-making terrorist hijacking of the Italian liner *Achille Lauro* (in the Eastern Med, in October 1985), the 15,000-ton *Stella Solaris* ("Star of the South") also had a temporary base at New York, running cruises to Bermuda, the Caribbean, and up to New England and Canada. She was also known for her periodic theme cruises, such as astronomy and theater-at-sea. Fine lecturers, which included well-known celebrities, such as Broadway and Hollywood stars, were often aboard. A rebuilt ship, she was actually quite moderate in size by current day standards, accommodating 730 passengers at maximum capacity. Her public rooms included a pleasant dining room, large main showroom, and lower-deck movie theater, while on deck, there was a large lido area with twin swimming pools. Her décor was Mediterranean modern, highlighted by Greek-themed works of art. Deep blue seemed to be a prevailing color, while wine-colored velour chairs seemed to be predominant in the lounges, bars, and restaurant.

"We made several cruises on the *Solaris* and enjoyed all of them," recalled Mr. and Mrs. Charles Fowler of Arizona:

> She was a pleasant ship, well run, but had an especially friendly spirit and happy crew. She was run by the Sun Line [which merged with the rival Epirotiki Lines in 1995 and together they became known as Royal Olympic Cruises] at the time and they had an excellent reputation. The Greek family owners looked after the ship much like you might look after a family yacht. Very little fell through the cracks. The ship had the most amazing crew, stewards and waiters and barmen that were onboard year after year, some for ten and even twenty years. They also had the most amazing memories, recalling not only your name and preferred drinks, but favorite items on the menu as well. There was a sort of magic, a Greek magic, to all of this. You felt, from the very first day, that you were at home, at a sort of favorite hotel where very little changed from year to year. Part of the great comfort of the *Stella Solaris* was in her great, unchanging consistency. You knew what to expect and it never, ever fell short. We made all sorts of cruises aboard, but our favorite was in November on a three-week trip from Greece and along the entire Mediterranean before crossing the mid-Atlantic to Caribbean ports and then finishing at Fort Lauderdale. There was such a contrast in this particular trip—from ports like Athens and Monte Carlo to San Juan and Nassau.

The *Stella Solaris* actually began sailing in the summer of 1953, but as the French passenger-cargo liner *Cambodge*. She had two twin sisters, the *Laos* and *Viet-Nam*, belonging to the Marseilles-based Messageries Maritimes. They were used on the long-haul service between Europe and the Far East. After departing from Marseilles, they passed through the Suez Canal and then called at Bombay and Colombo (on Ceylon) before heading to the likes of Singapore, Saigon, Manila, Hong Kong, Kobe, and Yokohama. Their passengers were diverse: from businessmen traveling to and from the East, the occasional tourist, traders and merchants, tea planters and silk buyers, missionaries, farm workers, and even French colonial soldiers and police forces. There were well-divided, classed accommodations onboard: upper-deck, highly comfortable first class, then second class, third class, and even fourth class, with all dormitory quarters. That Far Eastern trade dried up, however, in the late '60s as airlines stole the passengers and big, new containerized cargo ships secured the cargos.

The Sun Line bought the out-of-work *Cambodge* in 1969, and with actual plans as yet uncertain, provisionally renamed the 21-knot, steam turbine-driven ship as the *Stella V*. At the time, the Company was strengthening its cruise fleet, and liners such as the *Stella Solaris*, a mere 3,000-tonner, was inadequate and so was sold to Middle Eastern interests to become a sheik's yacht. In due course, the former *Cambodge* was gutted, extensively rebuilt, and then introduced as the "new" *Stella Solaris* in June 1973. She was then the largest Greek cruise ship sailing regularly on seven-night cruises from Piraeus. A gamble at first, she was soon a great success, indeed an affirmation of the increasing popularity of the Eastern Mediterranean and Greek isles. Along with her many other voyages, she did indeed give very worthwhile, very successful service over the years.

In September 2003, the 530-foot-long *Stella Solaris* was sold for scrapping to Indian buyers. Her last trip, with just a few crewmembers aboard, took her from Piraeus and through the Suez Canal to the remote beaches of Alang, near Mumbai, where she was deliberately run aground and then quickly invaded by $1-a-day demolition crews. She was said to be a "tired ship" in the end, her machinery all but worn out. She had a long life, of course, having been fifty years old.

Lighted and Aglow: The very popular *Stella Solaris* anchored off Mykonos. (*Sun Line*)

18

ON THE ROCKS: CRUISING MISHAPS

The *Ocean Princess* was a popular cruise ship in the 1980s, and her owners, Ocean Cruise Lines, were increasingly successful with some loyal followers. They also ran a second ship, the smaller *Ocean Islander*. The Fort Lauderdale-headquartered Company was expanding, especially with new itineraries.

Cruises to South America, including around the Straits of Magellan and into the exotic Amazon River, were increasingly popular in the '80s and seen, at least by some cruising regulars, as appealing alternatives to the saturated, wintertime Caribbean. Ocean Cruise Lines wanted to tap into that market and so used their largest and best ship, the 12,000-ton, 470-passenger *Ocean Princess*. Historically, that sleek ship had been built in 1967, but owned by the Italians and first chartered to then new Princess Cruises and marketed as the *Princess Italia*. Costa bought her in 1973 and then sailed her as the *Italia* before Ocean Cruise Lines grabbed her in 1980. She then became the *Ocean Princess*, cruising the Caribbean in wintertime and then sailing on Mediterranean and North European itineraries for the remainder of the year. But her days were almost ended, however, when in she nearly sank in Brazilian waters in March 1993. Dr. James Merrill was among her passengers at the time.

"We were 4½ days into an Amazon River cruise, having just left Belem," he remembered:

> As we left Belem harbor, we started to list and quite suddenly. It felt peculiar. The ship swung toward shore. It was all quite confusing. But then we learned the ship was taking on water in the theater on a lower deck. While we were told that there was no immediate danger, we were ordered to immediately go to our cabins, collect our lifejackets and proceed to the lifeboat stations. The ship was soon beached, stopped completely and quite still. No one was allowed below the Lido Deck and the watertight doors were closed. One woman was caught in the shower and others were in their swim suits. Certain cabins, the crew later announced, were safe and together we used flashlights to "throw" everything into suitcases. A local car ferry was brought alongside and the 300 passengers were sent to Belem, to the local Hilton Hotel. Another 60 of us, all in the American Express group, were sent to a smaller hotel.

"Passengers had left hurriedly, leaving clothes, jewelry and medications behind,' added Dr. Merrill:

> The ship's doctor was later supposed to help with medications, but never did. One entertainer lost all of his puppets. Another lost his guitar. Much later, there was some help. Passports were collected from the beached, half-sunk ship, and returned to each of us. Ocean Cruise Lines wanted to bring in a charter plane, from a one-plane airline, to bring us to the United States, but the Brazilian Government insisted that a Brazilian plane be used. Each of us was given a free ticket. When we finally left, the *Ocean Princess* was lying a few hundred yards from shore, aground and was already being stripped by the locals.

While the ship had hit river bed in the Amazon and began flooding, and while she was later abandoned and declared a "constructive loss," the vessel was actually transferred to a salvage company for removal and then for local scrapping, but was in fact resold to Greek owners known as Ellis Marine. Scared in rust and thick mud, she was carefully towed across the Atlantic to Piraeus in the summer of 1993, and where I later saw her, laid-up and being further stripped of her passenger fittings. Small mountains of velour lounge and dining room chairs, for example, sat on the pier side on that sizzling August afternoon. A different area included stacks of stateroom mattresses. Another liner, the former Soviet *Alexandr Pushkin*, was at the adjacent dock, being rebuilt and refurbished as the *Marco Polo*. The former *Ocean Princess* was now renamed *Sea Prince I*. Later, she was sold to Louis Cruise Lines, a then new cruise line interested in Eastern Mediterranean itineraries, and renamed *Princesa Oceanica*. Still later, in 1996, she was placed on charter to Britain's Thomson Holidays and renamed *Sapphire*. Later used on charter to France Croisieres as well, she has now long since returned to Louis Cruise Lines' use and, by 2007, was sailing from Nice on cruises around the western Mediterranean. The Sapphire was retired in 2010 and then scrapped in India two years later.

Above: The *Achille Lauro* burning to death off East Africa in December 1994. (*Author's collection*)

Left: Mishap: Costa's *Columbus* sank her pier at Cadiz, Spain, in August 1984. (*Author's collection*)

19

HOLIDAYS AT SEA: SANTA ON THE LIDO DECK

It is the annual Christmas–New Year cruise, that two-week escape from Miami to sun-drenched ports in the Caribbean, Colombia, Honduras, Belize, and Mexico. It is always very, very popular and so the *Crystal Serenity* sits perhaps a tad more deeply in these emerald green waters—there are 1,104 passengers onboard yet somehow fitted into the twelve-deck-high-ship's 1,060 official berths. The guests are indeed colorful, eager, mostly rich, and sometimes very rich. Evidently, there has been some last-minute shopping as well. At Christmas Eve, the classy jewel shop on Six Deck sold a diamond and sapphire necklace. The receipt showed $312,000, which an indulgent Mexican wanted—it was reported through the ship's ever-active grapevine—as a stocking-stuffer for his wife.

'There are lots of family reunions and get-togethers on these Holiday cruises,' according to the ship's Hotel Director:

> There is this great sense of pride in being together and in sharing. Sometimes it is a once-in-a-lifetime reunion. Others do it every year, always at Thanksgiving or at Christmas. Some parents take different kids or different grandkids on each trip. But other passengers are alone. Some come just to be with others, even strangers. Some come to avoid depression, that high sentimentality of the Holidays. The passengers and crew become a surrogate family. Still others come just to escape. One couple has just lost their fifty-two-year-old daughter to cancer. She was their only child. So, the loss at Christmas is especially heavy. Hopefully, the ship and the cruise help somewhat.

The *Crystal Serenity* is often more about the guests—never mere passengers on this moving palace—and they often outshine the ports of call. Many of them are older, of course. One ninety-four-year-old lady is in fact traveling all by her lonesome. The Los Angeles-based *Crystal Serenity* is often said to be "Rodeo Drive at sea—and the calling card is a gold Rolex!" But then there is also the Prada handbags, Manolo Blahnik shoes, and the golf ball-sized diamond rings. Formal nights are all but ablaze with sparkles, shimmers, and reflections. Half of Boca Raton is aboard along with touches of Palm Beach and Miami Beach, and maybe a sprinkling of Naples (also in Florida). There's also 100 Brits and fifty cheerful Mexicans. A friend onboard introduced us to a Mrs. Parker. Seems she is the Mrs. Parker of Parker-Meridian Hotels.

The ship is busy, a tad crowded in places, and the normally faultless service level pressed at times. From early morning, you all but have to book a chair on the otherwise spacious sun deck. Vuitton leather sacks and Gucci purses litter the place. Waiters scurry with trays of chilled Perrier and mango iced tea. The sun beats down as well as creamed and very oiled bodies begin to go toasty. You can scan this "moving Riviera" from the sports deck just above. Noticeably, lots of the ladies have a similar, almost confusing look. "Well, of course, they look alike," said blonde-wigged Thelma of Boca Pines (Florida). "After all, they've all been to the same plastic surgeon in the last year or so!" Conversations often lean toward, say, the best surgeon these days for south Florida nose jobs. With her half-dozen gold bracelets clattering, Thelma added, "It's all about beating the clock—erasing time. Today's eighty-five-year-old women want to look, well, sixty-five or at least seventy!"

Within, the ship looks like some upscale shopping mall—$250,000 in decorations have been brought onboard. There are elves, snowmen, even Santa on a motorcycle, but a tasteful, fun, bright red motorcycle. One guest noted: "The decorations are excellent as well as all-encompassing. Every holiday is considered. There is this sense of inclusion. There's even a Father Christmas, hinting of cruises past." The 20-foot-high tree in the lobby was ceremoniously lighted last night. A smartly-dressed couple (from West Palm, I am told) pressed the light-up button. Loyalists to that last bowl of caviar, they have made 106 Crystal cruises in sixteen years!

There was midnight mass, carols on deck and a well-timed arrival in Willemstad on Curacao (together with four other cruise ships) early on Wednesday morning.

Above: Cunard's legendary *QE2*, the most successful and widely traveled liner of all time. (*Author's collection*)

Right: When it was commissioned in March 1977 at New York, the 17,000-ton *Cunard Princess* was said to be "the last cruise ship to be built." The industry, it was then believed, had ebbed out. (*Author's collection*)

Above left: Princess Grace of Monaco did the naming honors. (*Author's collection*)

Above right: The mighty *Queen Mary 2*, seen here at her inaugural cruise season, in February 2004, at Rio de Janeiro. (*Cunard Line*)

Below left: Japan entered the U.S. and international cruise markets with luxurious Crystal Cruises in 1990. (*Crystal Cruises*)

Below right: Radisson Cruise Lines added the catamaran-style *Radisson Diamond*. (*Radisson Cruises*)

20

GROWTH AND EVOLUTION: PRINCESS CRUISES TURNS FIFTY!

In 2015, Los Angeles-based Princess Cruises turned fifty! Indeed, it has been a very successful "voyage." Seattle-based businessman Stanley McDonald started it all by chartering the little, 6,000-ton, 350-bed *Princess Patricia*, normally used on the May–October run from Vancouver up to Alaska. Not an official cruise ship (she lacked the likes of air-conditioning, an outdoor pool, and private bathrooms in most of her cabins), she sat idle, however, in the winter months. Mr. McDonald wanted to join the budding North American cruise industry and so chartered the *Princess Patricia*, beginning in December 1965, for an experimental season of winter cruising to the "new" Mexican Riviera—from Los Angeles southward on sunny voyages to the likes of Acapulco, Puerto Vallarta, and Mazatlan. He named his new venture for the *Princess Patricia*—Princess Cruises was in business and the experiment paid off.

By 1967, he chartered the larger, better-equipped, sleek-looking, 500-passenger *Italia* and ran her as the *Princess Italia* (she was actually never officially renamed). Things moved quickly: he was soon chartering a third ship Costa's *Carla "C"* (the former French Line *Flandre*) by 1968 and advertised her as the *Princess Carla*. Itineraries expanded as well—to Alaska in summers and added Trans-Panama Canal cruises in winter. Princess was so successful that, by 1974, it caught the eye of Britain's mighty P&O Lines. Three fine ships were by now owned outright: the *Pacific Princess*, *Island Princess*, and *Sun Princess* (ex-*Spirit of London* of P&O). Then a stroke of immense good fortune: the 650-passenger *Pacific Princess* was, beginning in 1975, used as the setting for the tremendously popular *Love Boat* television series. Running for over a decade and being seen each week by as many as 40 million Americans, it was in itself a great spark to the growth of mass-market cruising. Each episode was said to be worth $10–12 million in advertising, which also benefited other cruise lines—in fact, the entire industry. The first purposeful brand-new Princess ship was the 44,000-grt *Royal Princess* (now the German-owned *Artania*), commissioned in 1984. Princess progressed and doubled its fleet in 1988 when it bought (for $200 million) rival Sitmar Cruises. A Sitmar new build of 1988, the 63,000-grt *Fairmajesty*, was completed instead as the 1,800-passenger *Star Princess*. In 2000, P&O-Princess Cruises was de-merged from the P&O group of companies, and three years later, it became part of the ever-expanding Carnival Group.

These days, Princess is bigger and more lucrative than ever—seventeen cruise liners that carry almost 1½ million passengers a year. The Company built two series of new ships in the 1990s: the 77,400-grt *Sun Princess* began one group of four and then was followed by a larger class led by the 107,000-grt, 3,200-passenger *Grand Princess*. The present fleet also includes the 115,000-grt sisters *Diamond Princess* and *Sapphire Princess*, both constructed by Mitsubishi Heavy Industries. Currently, the Italian-built, 142,000-grt *Royal Princess* and her sister *Regal Princess* are the Company's newest and largest liners. A third and then a fourth sister, the *Majestic Princess* and *Sky*

Princess, followed in 2017–19. The current Princess motto: "Warm, elegant service in an atmosphere of comfortable elegance."

Myself, I have sailed on about fifteen Princess cruises, including the original *Pacific Princess* as well as the year-old *Royal Princess*. On that most recent voyage, I could not have been more pleased. It was in fact one of my best cruises. After a week onboard (from New York north to Canada and New England), I found the five best features of the giant *Royal Princess*, they might be in this order:

1. Great, very discernible friendliness of the entire staff and crew.
2. Overall service—everywhere and anywhere onboard.
3. High food quality and diversity.
4. Array of amenities and services.
5. Overall entertainment.

What a great company and grand fleet. Happy birthday, Princess!

21

SPECIAL OCCASIONS: RENDEZVOUS OF THE CUNARD QUEENS

There are no more famous ocean liners, we think, than the Cunard Queens. There have been five to date and a sixth on the way (the 90,000-ton *Queen Victoria*, was due out in December 2007). Just about everyone remembers the *Queen Mary* and *Queen Elizabeth*—that original 1930s pair that sailed the North Atlantic for years and in glorious tandem. They were the most popular and successful pair of Atlantic super liners ever. The *Mary* was actually the more beloved and not only by passengers, but by staff as well. It was said that she not only had a certain grandeur, a mystique, but something given to but a few ships: she had a "soul." This transcended to those onboard. The *Queen Elizabeth 2*, the now much-beloved *QE2*, followed in 1969 as something of a royal successor, but actually quite a breakaway in many ways, including design and decoration. Given almost icon status these days, she is thought to be a grand example of what is now called "mid-century" style, and having sailed for thirty-nine years, she has broken every superliner record—more miles sailed, more passengers carried, just about more everything. Then, in 2003, came the *Queen Mary 2*, the largest, tallest, most costly build liner to date. She had, it seems, almost instant celebrity.

The *Queens* always seem to be making news, but in February 2006, on a rather magical Australian summer's evening in Sydney, Cunard could not have even wished for a more successful occasion. The two *Queens*—the *QE2* and the *QM2*—met while traveling westward on their respective world cruises. We had arrived that morning to a joyous, spirited reception aboard the 1,132-foot-long *Mary 2*. Although a Tuesday and so a normal work day, the crowds along the shores were huge. Hundreds of boats serenaded the liner from daybreak onwards, just after we passed through the famed Sydney Heads. Helicopters and small planes buzzed overhead, fireboats sprayed, and all while whistles, horns, and sirens created a seemingly endless concert. Onboard, the outer, upper decks were crowded with passengers and crew alike. Slowly, the 151,000-ton *Queen* made her way into the harbor, passed that grand Opera House, and then, with easy precision, turned just before the Harbor Bridge, reversed course, and then slowly docked in a specially prepared berth at the naval dock yard on Garden Island. She was simply too big, too long, to use the normal passenger berth at Circular Quay, located just across from the Opera House. Once ashore, the 2,500 or so passengers (including 800 Australians) were bussed across downtown Sydney to a cruise terminal in Darling Harbor for final disembarkation.

We had joined the $800 million, seventeen-deck-high *Queen Mary 2* two weeks earlier, in another favorite port-city: San Francisco. From a shoreline jetty, we watched as she made her mid-afternoon arrival, a sort of royal procession, and in glorious, golden California sunshine. Again, hundreds of small boats, chartered craft, ferries, and more of those spouting fireboats created the royal court. Included was the flag-bedecked, splendidly preserved World War II Liberty ship *Jeremiah O'Brien*. She was almost top-heavy with 900 onboard, many of them loyalist subscribers to saving that sixty-three-year-old vessel. Tens of thousands, so television new casters reported, lined the waterfront near Pier 29 and then well into the night just to see the largest Atlantic Ocean liner ever built. Her funnel and uppermost lights were switched off, however, to comply with a City rule that no tall, lighted structure can compete with the nocturnal skyline. The next day, at a gala luncheon, the *QM2* was officially welcomed by the mayor and other officials. That night, we sailed—with appropriate touches of the famed San Francisco fog and the tooting of a few deep-voiced horns—and headed-off on a fifteen-night trip to Honolulu, Pago Pago, Auckland, and finally Sydney. "It is a dream come true to sail on the *Queen Mary 2* and on her maiden world cruise and on her maiden calls to Pago Pago, Auckland and Sydney," said a British couple from Bath. "My father had been a soldier during the Second World War and went overseas on the original *Queen Mary* and my mother went to America for a visit in the 1950s on the *Queen Elizabeth*, and so this is a wonderful connection to them."

Auckland laid on a very spirited early morning reception for the 28-knot *QM2* and later city streets were clogged, often brought to a standstill, as Saturday afternoon crowds flocked to the waterfront to see the mighty Cunarder. The ten-hour visit ended with a one-hour fireworks extravaganza and more of those small boats and tooting tugboats as we sailed for Australia and an even grander reception. Australia did, indeed, lay out the thickest, grandest red carpet.

Sydney newspapers and television news were ablaze with the *QM2*'s arrival. She was not just headlines, but big headlines. Some Australians remembered, of course, that wartime meeting of the original *Mary* and *Elizabeth*, then both in troopship gray, off those Sydney Heads back in January 1941. Afterward, for a year or so, the converted *Queens* carried Aussie soldiers off to war, mostly across the Indian Ocean to Suez for the Allied reinforcement of North Africa and the Middle East.

Throughout the day, there were luncheons, tours, special tea parties, and a long string of televised tours and interviews with top staff members onboard the *QM2*. Yet an even bigger, greater occasion was just hours away. At 7 p.m., as Sydney skies were slowly, evocatively turning from golden hues to cinnamon and finally to charcoal, we boarded a friend's large cabin cruiser and joined an estimated 500 other craft in the outer harbor. With the towering *QM2* still berthed at the naval dock yard (and sailing that night, close to midnight, for Hong Kong), the majestic *QE2* arrived, flag-bedecked and sounding her throaty, big liner whistles. Again, small craft formed the royal procession. Horns and sirens again sounded continuously, and those fireboats sent up their great watery fans. Off the naval pier, the 70,000-ton *Elizabeth* seemed to pause, as if to pay homage, a sort of royal curtsey, queen mother to queen so to speak, to her larger successor. With their whistles, they exchanged greetings. They had, in fact, been together a month before, in mid-January, as they sailed together from Fort Lauderdale. Then, slowly, graciously, now beginning to light from end to end, the *Elizabeth* made her way toward the Harbor Bridge, passing the floodlit Opera House and then, with tugboat assistance, was swung round, the front of her 963-foot long hull pointed outward and berthed at Circular Quay, the main passenger terminal. It was all perfectly timed, choreographed as if a part of the royal ballet, and then finished off with a blazing fireworks show (some said "the greatest ever in Sydney harbor"). Two million were reportedly along the shores or on boats and there were subsequent traffic jams, going well into the wee hours, which took hours to sort. But in all, it was a grand occasion, a thoroughly memorable travel experience and a gala meeting of the world's two most famous liners. Cunard must have been thrilled.

Above left: The fabled *QE2* meets her "big sister," the *Queen Mary 2*, at Sydney in February 2007. (*Cunard Line*)

Above right: Three *Queens*: Cunard's 175th anniversary in 2015 and their three liners met at Liverpool. *Queen Elizabeth* (top), *Queen Mary 2* (middle), and *Queen Victoria* (bottom). (*Cunard Line*)

Left: Eight P&O cruise ships departed in formation from Southampton on a July afternoon in 2012. It was the Company's 175th anniversary. (*P&O*)

Elizabeth II was celebrating sixty years as queen up in London, but the three Cunard *Queens* met at Southampton to add to the occasion. (*Cunard Line*)

It was "Cunard Day" in Manhattan: The three *Queens* departing from New York on a bitterly cold January night in 2011. (*Cunard Line*)

22

"LIVING" ON THE LINERS

"There's nothing quite like being onboard a ship, a moving hotel," said a couple with over 200 cruises to their credit and all aboard six-star Crystal Cruises. Others agree. Japanese-owned, Los Angeles-based Crystal seems the perfect sea-going residence. Recently, it was revealed that at least four women were "living" aboard the *Crystal Symphony*. Indeed, it became their "home." Some have actually sold off their shore-side residences, and then, only when necessary, move to a hotel if, say, a ship itself goes off to dry dock. Others stay aboard for ten and eleven months of the year. Itineraries and ports of call are often less important, some say, but instead, it is simply the very comfortable, very luxurious lifestyle aboard ships such as the 950-berth *Symphony*. One lady with 150 Crystal cruises under her belt added, "It is like living in the best hotel in the world except that it moves!"

In bygone cruising days, Clara McBeth was (and remains) the all-time champion. For an extraordinary fourteen years, she "lived" aboard Cunard's legendary "Green Goddess": the *Caronia*, a ship dubbed "the millionaires' yacht" and which did little else other than cruising the world. Miss McBeth, it was estimated, spent $5 million in 1950s dollars. She had a two-room suite, thought of the 34,000-ton ship as "her yacht," and, in later years, rarely went ashore. Once a week, the captain came to her suite—for afternoon tea.

There were others. When Beatrice Muller first went to sea some twenty years ago, she was a virtual novice to ocean liners and to cruising. Yet she was soon "hooked"—and "line and sinker" too! Although now passed away, she had been "living" aboard the iconic *Queen Elizabeth 2* for nine years. She was, without question, then the world champ of cruise loyalists.

The subject of almost countless television and radio interviews, newspaper and magazine articles, featured in maritime books, and herself the star of a segment on television's newsy weekly *Sixty Minutes*, Bea was madly in love with the legendary *QE2* and sailed on hundreds of voyages, crossings, and cruises alike.

The ship was retired from active service in November 2008, indeed like some old, long-serving sailor (thirty-nine years in all, and creating more records than any other big liner in history), and has gone off to a new life out in Dubai. Bea was, of course, aboard for the final hours, seeing the Cunard and the British flags hauled down and the official signing over to her new Mid-Eastern owners. "I was heartsick, of course," said the energetic Bea, an official resident of Somerville in central New Jersey, but then more realistically something of an "international citizen." We sailed together for the last time, in October 2008, in the wake of many prior trips together. It was truly a truly sentimental journey: the *Elizabeth*'s Farewell to the British Isles cruise and then the Last Westbound Crossing to New York.

"The *QE2* has been my home off and on, but mostly on, for the past fourteen years—but nine years fulltime!" she said with a proud smile as we sipped and ate our way through one of those elegant white glove teas in the splendors of the Queens Room aboard the 70,000-ton

Elizabeth 2. "There is no ship like the *QE2* and there never, ever will be again," she added nostalgically:

> But now, I have to find a new home. I am going to cry a lot. But I am going next [in December] to the *Queen Victoria*, for a Mediterranean cruise, and try to "live" at 21 knots (the ever-powerful *QE2* could, when pushed, top 32 knots) and then on the 100-night world cruise of the *Queen Mary 2*. But mostly, I will miss the wonderful personnel and fellow passengers aboard the *QE2*. We were like a family. And the *QE2* gave me up to forty-eight ports of call each year. Yes, I will miss the *QE2*. But sadly, nothing is forever!

Exploration and small ship cruising on Hapag-Lloyd's *Hanseatic*. (*Hapag-Lloyd*)

Above left: Cruising over the North Pole on a Russian icebreaker. (*Author's collection*)

Above right: Mud Pie and Banjo Music: Cruising the American rivers on the classic *Delta Queen*. (*Delta Queen Steamboat Co.*)

Left: Grand style on the far newer *American Queen*. (*Delta Queen Steamboat Co.*)

Above left: Casual living on a Mississippi riverboat. (*Delta Queen Steamboat Co.*)

Above right: European river cruising has become extremely popular and had expanded considerably by 2015. (*Author's collection*)

Right: Cruising from China—exploding in popularity by 2015—was started by such ships as the *Yaohua* in the 1970s. (*Author's collection*)

Above left: Japan had a cruise ship, the *Shin Sakura Maru*, which was aimed at teenagers—they learned while they cruised. (*Hisashi Noma collection*)

Above right: In the 1980s, the Dutch experimented with a "no frills" cruise ship, the *Vacationer*, seen here at Cadiz. (*Author's collection*)

Left: Cargo ships can carry up to twelve passengers—no doctor is thereby required. Freighter travel has had revival, and by 2010, over 300 ships worldwide were listed as carrying two to twelve passengers. (*Author's collection*)

Above left: Older cruise ships had long histories and often many names. The 1944-built *Emerald Seas* had some fifteen names before she was retired. (*Author's collection*)

Above right: Sitmar's *Fairsea* had been Cunard's *Carinthia* in her first life. (*Author's collection*)

Right: The *Regal Empress* had been the Greek *Olympia* and later the *Caribe*. *(Author's collection)*

23

AGING GRACEFULLY: SOME OLDER CRUISE SHIPS

Shipbuilders could not know, but some ships they built go on forever—for decades and decades. It is good, solid construction, but probably a matter of fate more than anything else. A prime example: the famed *Queen Elizabeth 2*, the iconic *QE2*, sailed for thirty-nine years. She sailed longer than any big liner in history. She was also the longest-serving ship in the 175 years of Cunard Line history, and the 70,000-ton *QE2* made other records: she carried more passengers, steamed more miles, visited more ports, and made more money than any other super liner in history. A Cunard officer once told me: "She was innovative, unique, lucky, and, most of all, very successful." These days, however, the *QE2* just waits out in Dubai. After being retired from Cunard service in November 2008, she was to have become a luxury residence, entertainment center, and collection of shops and restaurants, and all while moored on the extravagant Palm Island. Plans did not materialize, however, and then other plans—being a hotel at Cape Town, being berthed in London and, most recently, being used as a moving hotel in Chinese and other Far Eastern ports—failed as well. The fate of the *QE2*, forty-eight years old in 2017, was uncertain. The ship finally opened as a moored hotel in April 2018. Another idle liner with an uncertain future, but at Philadelphia, is the record-breaking speed queen *United States*. She was sixty-five years old in 2017.

There are other, if less famous, deep-sea passenger ships that endure. The Portuguese-owned *Astoria*, still cruising on charter, is nearly seventy years old. Completely rebuilt and modernized by the early 1990s, the strong and solid hull dates back to 1948 when the 15,000-ton ship was first commissioned as the Swedish American Line's *Stockholm*. She has had many changes and more than six different names since then. The *Hikawa Maru*, a museum ship at Yokohama, dates from 1930, and the *Rotterdam*, another floating museum (at Rotterdam), was first completed in 1959. Of course, there is the grande dame of all museum and hotel ships, the *Queen Mary*. Moored at Long Beach, near Los Angeles, the last three-funnel ocean liner (and one that crossed the Atlantic 1,000 times and sailed for Cunard for thirty-one years) will turn eighty next year.

Yet oldest of all of these passenger ships might just be the *Doulos Phos*. In 2018, the little 6,800-ton ship turned 104, and she is a part of current cruising history as well. Back in 1914, the Newport News Shipbuilding & Dry Dock Company in Virginia (and where, among others, the super ship *United States* was constructed) launched a small, unnoticed freighter, the *Medina*. Completed on the eve of World War I, she was built for an American ship owner, the long-gone Mallory Lines, for U.S. inter-coastal freight services. Fortunately, she survived both world wars but was then put up for sale in 1948. Already being over thirty years of age, she might have been scrapped. Instead, she was sold—for a low price—to European shipping operators, who used a "flag of convenience" subsidiary, the Panama-flag Compania Naviera San Miguel. With the pressing post-World War II need to transport migrants, refugees, and displaced persons out of Europe, she was rebuilt as the austere immigrant ship *Roma*.

Her cargo holds were made over as dormitories, holding as many as 850 at full capacity. A long-ago friend at New York visited the ship soon afterward and described her quarters as being "close to turn-of-the-century steerage."

Tens of thousands of Europeans wanted a new post-war life—mostly for economic reasons—and looked to the likes of the United States, Canada, South America, Australia, and South Africa for resettlement. Under charter, the *Roma* was sent off on crowded, often cramped voyages, mostly from Genoa and Naples to Rio de Janeiro and Buenos Aires and, farther afield, to Melbourne and Sydney. In 1950, she was chartered by a religious organization for cheap travel between New York and the Mediterranean for the special Holy Year celebrations in Rome. The two-week crossings were priced from $110.

In the early '50s, the Genoa-based Costa Line was beginning to expand its passenger ship business, begun for them in 1947 and linked to Latin America, and so, in 1952, bought the small, aged *Roma*. Obviously, they saw potential in her strongly-built, American hull. She was refitted and improved as the *Franca "C,"* busily carrying more immigrants between Naples, Genoa, Cannes, Barcelona, and Lisbon and then across to Rio de Janeiro, Santos, Montevideo, and Buenos Aires. Her westward trips were booked to capacity. Costa soon added more passenger ships.

In 1959, and now despite her forty-five years, the 410-foot-long *Franca "C"* was thoroughly rebuilt as a high-standard cruise ship by Costa, upgraded and even re-engined (with new Fiat diesels). In her new guise, she looked sleek, modern, and certainly age-defying. Evidently, there was still more life (and profit) in the little ship. Costa sent her off on Mediterranean cruises, to the Adriatic, Greek isles, and, on occasion, to the Black Sea and West Africa. She now carried up to 354 passengers, all in air-conditioned, brightly colored, comfortable cabins, and all of them with private bathroom facilities. She had a series of new public rooms, all done in tasteful Mediterranean modern decor, a showroom, dining room, and umbrella-lined lido deck complete with kidney bean-shaped swimming pool.

By the early '60s, the *Franca "C"* began to spend her winters at Port Everglades in Florida. Then an infant cruise port, the ship was scheduled for Caribbean cruises from three to fourteen days. A three-night cruise (to Nassau and Freeport) was priced from $59 or less than $20 per person per day. Years later, in 1968, while sailing from San Juan, Puerto Rico, the *Franca "C"* inaugurated the first air-sea combination sailings. Cruise lines and air lines hereafter became friends. Near the end of her Costa days, in the mid '70s, the ship was kept closer to home, cruising from Venice to Adriatic and Aegean ports. Almost deservedly, she was laid-up in winter, and then, in 1977, she was seemingly out of service forever.

A year later, in 1978, the *Franca "C"* (then sixty-four years old) found yet more life—as a floating missionary book and evangelical center. It was in this role that I visited her as the renamed *Doulos*, registered in Malta but with German owners at Tenerife in the summer of 1983. She sailed for Operation Mobilization, created in the 1960s to promote Christian brotherhood and distribute literature. When I visited, the ship had been converted with permanent exhibit space for as many as 4,000 books. Even the outdoor and lido deck were used. Additionally, another 500,000 books were said to be in the ship's holds. The staff of 300—from the captain to the last assistant cook and greaser—worked as volunteers. The ship sailed the world.

New, strict safety maritime safety regulations finally spelled the end for the *Doulos* (then eighty-five years old) in 2009. A refit and upgrading would have cost $15 million. In 2010, the *Doulos* was sold to Singapore buyers, who planned to preserve the ship for use at resort on the Indonesian island of Bintan. The plans included installation of a restaurants, wine and juice bars, a bookshop, meeting rooms, a maritime museum, and, in reflection of her past, a bible school. The ship's hull and steel were later reinforced and strengthened, and then, using chains and lifting equipment, the vessel was pulled-up a hillside, overlooking Bintan harbor. The *Doulos* has been renamed as the *Doulos Phos* ("Servant of Light").

Some ships just seem to endure forever.

Above left: The *QE2* arrived in Dubai in November 2008 and has remained there ever since. (*Author's collection*)

Above right: Italy's *Valtur Prima* has survived. She has been sailing for nearly seventy years, and she began her long career as Sweden's *Stockholm*, built in 1948. (*Author's collection*)

Below left: One plan for the *QE2* was to see her used as a floating hotel in China but moving periodically from port to port. (*Cunard Line*)

Below right: Waiting: The *QE2* in Dubai in April 2016. (*Author's collection*)

24

FROM HAMBURG TO VENICE: EUROPEAN CRUISING

By the 1990s, European cruising was already booming. Within twenty years (by 2017), Germany was the second largest cruise market in the world (second only to North America and having outpaced the U.K.) and while the likes of Germany's Aida Cruises and Italy's Costa and MSC Cruises were expanding with their biggest, splashiest, most sophisticated ships yet. The European market (for cruises from the likes of seven nights to the Aegean, fourteen days to Norway and the Baltic, or fly-sail cruises from Barbados, Durban, Dubai, and Shanghai) are hugely popular. Europeans are all running to book cruises, and primarily for its excellent value.

Europe was once, say fifty years ago, in the '60s, the domain of mostly older, second and third hand, modestly refitted passenger ships. The demands (by passengers) were all but minimal. Yet gradually, both the European and British markets expanded, and with that demands for bigger and certainly better liners took hold.

Costa Cruises is perhaps the biggest of the European operators. Founded in 1924 with freighters, the Genoa-based firm began carrying passengers, Italian migrants mostly, just after World War II, in 1947–48. Their first liners were the 12,000-ton *Anna "C"* and a converted freighter, the 8,000-ton *Andrea "C."* Business flourished, and in 1959, they added fulltime cruising to their scope with the 354-passenger *Franca "C."* Her voyages included winter trips from then emerging Port Everglades in Florida and later, by 1968, included the first fly-cruise operations ($150 for flights to and from New York and a three-night cruise from Florida to the Bahamas). Costa had, by the late 1970s, the largest passenger ship fleet apart from that of the Soviet Union. In 1996, a 50-percent share of the Company was bought by Carnival Corporation, and by 2001, Carnival had full ownership. By 2017, Costa was at its all-time peak: fifteen large cruise ships and several on order. With worldwide itineraries, Costa has been a major investor in the rapidly expanding Chinese cruise market and this has included a fully-booked world cruise to and from Shanghai.

MSC Cruises is also Italian, having been formed as a freight line in 1969. Today a huge container ship operator (with over 400 ships) and ranking as the largest privately-owned shipping firm, MSC entered the cruise business in 1987 when it acquired Lauro Line's *Achille Lauro*, which was soon restyled under the banner of Star Lauro Cruises. Business prospered, several secondhand passenger ships were gradually added, and by 1995, the Company was renamed MSC Cruises. With twelve large, newly-built cruise ships in service by 2016, as many as eight additional liners are planned into the 2020s.

Also one of Europe's largest and most popular cruise lines, Germany's AIDA Cruises has also had great expansion. With twelve liners in service by 2017, the Company has roots back to 1991 when it began with a single ship, the *Arkona*. Britain's P&O later invested and then joined with Germany's Seetours to form AIDA Cruises in 1999. Then with the merger of P&O with Carnival-owned Princess in 2003, AIDA came under Carnival control. AIDA was moved, however, to a Carnival subsidiary, Costa Cruises, managed from Genoa (but later moved back to Germany). AIDA has been described as "Cruise ships that cater to the German-speaking market. And as seagoing 'club resorts,' AIDA ships have on-board amenities and facilities designed to attract younger, more active vacationers."

Britain's P&O Cruises is another significant operator with eight liners in 2017. It is the biggest cruise line in the U.K., the third largest cruise market in the world. P&O is also the most historic, dating back to 1837 and the formation of the Peninsular Steam Navigation Co. (later the Peninsular & Oriental Steam Navigation Co., best known as P&O). Primarily interested in passenger service to Spain, Portugal, and the Mediterranean, the first cruise was offered in 1844 and the first proper cruise ship, the 150-passenger *Vectis*, was added in 1904. P&O has grown steadily since—the Company had 197 ships on the eve of World War I, in 1914. In addition to expansive services to the likes of India, Australia, and the Far East, P&O became a well-known British cruise line. Alone, in 1929, fifteen cruises were offered from London as well as Southampton, but as the traditional liner services faded by the 1970s, P&O became P&O Cruises and turned almost entirely to cruising, from Southampton as well as Sydney. P&O Cruises and P&O-owned Princess Cruises became independent from the larger P&O Steam Navigation Company in 2000. Three years later, when it might have been sold to Royal Caribbean, P&O Princess became part of Carnival. Along with Cunard, P&O is a primary part of Southampton-based Carnival U.K.

European and British cruising has supported many other if smaller cruise lines such as Fred Olsen, Saga, Cruise & Maritime Voyages, Phoenix Reisen, Hapag-Lloyd, Louis Cruises, Ponant, Pullmantur, TUI, Thomson, and others.

Hapag-Lloyd's *Europa* was said to be the "most luxurious" liner afloat in the 1980s. (*Hapag-Lloyd*)

Right: MSC Cruises' huge *MSC Fantasia*—carrying up to 4,300 passengers—is seen at Tunis. (*Author's collection*)

Below: German Visitor: The *AIDAluna* at New York in September 2016. (*Author's collection*)

25

BIGGER AND BIGGER: *OASIS OF THE SEAS* AND *ALLURE OF THE SEAS*

Shipyard designers, artisans, and, of course, workers themselves have begun the creation, at the STX Shipyard at St. Nazaire, France, of what will be the biggest, tallest, longest, and widest passenger liner ever. Named *Harmony of the Seas*, the 227,700 tonner was built for the world's second largest cruise operator, Royal Caribbean International, and was out in the summer of 2016. There is more exciting news: there will be a sister and possibly a third and even a fourth version. A follow-up to the highly successful, 225,300-ton, 6,400-bed *Oasis of the Seas* and *Allure of the Seas*, this new liner is aimed at the biggest, busiest cruise market anywhere: the Caribbean. She will do seven-night itineraries.

When I was a boy, back in the 1950s, and following the comings and goings of ocean liners at New York harbor, transatlantic liners were the biggest and mightiest yet. In 1955, for example, Britain's Cunard Line had the two largest: the 83,600-ton *Queen Elizabeth* and the 81,200-ton *Queen Mary*. The order then dropped quickly to the 53,300-ton *United States* and then the 51,800-ton *Liberte*. It seemed that no liner would ever surpass them. Even two flashy newcomers of the '60s failed to surpass them: the 66,000-ton *France* (1962) and then the 65,000-ton *Queen Elizabeth 2* (1969). The 1,035-foot-long *France* did, however, surpass the *Queen Elizabeth* by 4 feet and ranked as the longest ocean liner ever built for the next forty years.

These days, we could not have imagined not only the staggering growth of the worldwide cruise industry, but the sheer size of cruise ships themselves. The *Oasis of the Seas* and her sister are, for example, nearly five times the size of the immortal *Titanic*, built over a century ago in 1912. In the current pecking order the 225,000-ton *Oasis* and *Allure* are followed by the 155,800-ton *Norwegian Epic* of another Miami-based firm, Norwegian Cruise Lines. NCL has, by the way, two larger ships, the *Norwegian Escape* and *Norwegian Bliss*, under construction for delivery in 2016 and 2017.

The 4,100-bed *Epic* is followed by more Royal Caribbean cruise tonnage: the 154,000-ton *Freedom of the Seas* and her two sisters, *Liberty of the Seas* and *Independence of the Seas*. Cunard's *Queen Mary 2*, said to be the last true "ocean liner" and which runs Atlantic crossings about half the year, is next largest and weighs in at 151,000 tons. After her, and just recently commissioned, are the 145,000-ton sisters *Norwegian Breakaway* and *Norwegian Getaway*. Princess Cruises pops up next with their 142,000-ton pair of *Royal Princess*, and, in 2017, the *Regal Princess*. Our list here concludes with two Italian-owned ships, MSC Cruises' *MSC Divina* and *MSC Preziosa*, both just short of 140,000 tons each.

But are even bigger ships coming? Besides the new Royal Caribbean mega-liners, even mighty Carnival does not have plans for larger cruise ships. Assuredly, with the cruise business growing and expanding throughout the world, larger liners will be coming on line.

Above: When it was completed in 1987, the 70,000-ton *Sovereign of the Seas* was the first newly built mega-sized cruise ship. She was just the beginning. (*Royal Caribbean Cruise Lines*)

Below: The dining room is three decks high. (*Royal Caribbean Cruise Lines*)

Right: The lobby of the *Sovereign of the Seas*. (*Royal Caribbean Cruise Lines*)

Above: The ice arena was a great novelty in 1999. (*Royal Caribbean Cruise Lines*)

Below: Hamburgers and Fries: A Johnny Rockets Diner up on the top deck. (*Royal Caribbean Cruise Lines*)

Left: A horizontal lobby—an arcade of shops, bars, and attractions. (*Royal Caribbean Cruise Lines*)

Above: The impressive main show room, with extraordinary shows. (*Royal Caribbean Cruise Lines*)

Below: In the mid-1980s, Sea Goddess Cruises became the most luxurious and expensive "small cruise ship" company. (*Sea Goddess Cruises*)

Right: The ship's funnel is also a rock-climbing wall. (*Royal Caribbean Cruise Lines*)

Dining on Sea Goddess was said to be exceptional. (*Sea Goddess Cruises*)

Seabourn Cruise Lines followed with two deluxe yacht-like cruise ships, which could use smaller ports. (*Seabourn Cruise Lines*)

26

SIX-STAR BRANDING: GOLD-PLATED CRUISING

Cruising is a divided business—big ship, high-capacity cruising, expedition cruising, educational cruising, and luxury cruising. In the summer of 2016, I joined Silversea Cruises' beautiful *Silver Whisper*, sparkling, yacht-like, and indulgently carrying only 375 "guests" while being looked after by 150 seemingly handpicked staff. Indeed, it was pure silver-plated cruising—the top of the six-star class of luxury ships! On our trip, we crossed the North Atlantic, departing from Southampton, England, and making three stops in Ireland and then calls in Iceland and Greenland, and finally several calls in Canada before finishing in Quebec City and Montreal. It was a grand and glorious voyage in every way!

For myself, it was something like my fifteenth trip with this Italian-owned, but Monte Carlo-based firm, and Silversea has prospered and grown. Altogether, the Company now has eight ships: four for luxury cruising, four for equally luxurious expedition cruising (an increasing popular alternate to, well, plain old, ordinary luxury cruising), and then, in the spring of 2017, the Line will bring out their biggest ship yet, the 596-guest, eight-restaurant *Silver Muse*. At Silversea headquarters, it seems they have been tweaking things, here and there, and why not—the high-end luxury market is growing, expanding, in fact booming. It is the top end of ocean travel, where guests have been just about everywhere, travel first class in the skies and sleep in the very best hotels and resorts ashore. So, at sea, they want the best, not glittery or razzmatazz luxury but that quiet, exacting atmosphere of a posh club. It must be all elegance, but quiet elegance. The guests themselves were a mix: half North American, almost half European, and then throw in a handful of South Africans and Australians.

The ship (built in 1999) had just had a refurbishment—some redecorating, redoing, and fixing. The service remains "hot & cold running butlers"—in immaculate uniforms and equally immaculate white gloves—and they have been to butler school. They do it all, including organizing your closet, putting your shoes in perfect, soldier-like order, fluffing your pillows (there are ten kinds, by the way, on the "pillow menu"), and "wave their magic wands." Anywhere and everywhere onboard, you are treated and accorded like the very top passenger—that golden regular with the most cruises. Smiles, gentle service, endless kindness, and attention are the orders of the day (and in the night, there is another, fully-uniformed "night butler" for that call at 2 a.m.—you just buzz him!).

The ship is all suites—no ordinary staterooms or cabins here—and so its bedroom (incredible mattresses matched with incredibly soft Italian linens), complete living room, picture windows, a desk/work area the size of Montana, massive marble, and glass baths and walk-in closets that would have been lower-deck, tourist class quarters on the likes of the old *Queen Mary* or *Île de France*.

Pots and pans: but it is the food which to me has had the biggest overhaul. It was always wonderful on Silversea—but now, let us say it is wonderfully superb! The new motto is simple: "quality over quantity," and the waiters now use iPads, which—with the entry of your suite number—instantly display the likes of your food restrictions and allergies. Yes, you are kindly, but softly reminded just in case. Of course, down to the last sugar cube, everything is splendidly served, on gleaming tableware and on brand-new, almost streamline silverware, washed down with fine wines and the portions deliberately smaller—you rarely, if ever, leave the dinner table feeling like the Goodyear blimp.

So here goes—a dinner menu: nine categories to start with: Crudo Bar, appetizers, soups, salads, pastas, "From the Sea," "From the Fields" (extra fresh and so extra healthy), gourmet burgers, and "From the Garden." Among several offerings, we turn to a mellow Chilean red wine (and even the wine steward steps off the pages of a glossy brochure—good looking, that French accent, aptly from Bordeaux!).

Let us start with an appetizer: fresh goat cheese and cherry tomato tian (and all done in a puff pastry). Then it is South East Asian lentil soup (lentils, carrots, leeks, celery, fennel, and Asian spices). Then on to a pasta course: homemade penne with fresh arugula, cherry tomatoes, garlic, aged parmesan, and a dash of olive oil. For the main course: beef bourguignon (braised black Angus beef bathed in red Burgundy, beef broth, a drizzle of garlic, pearl onions, mushrooms, and all resting on a bed of creamy mash potatoes). If the waiter (impeccably trained and from Chennai in India) insists, a side of black tiger prawn curry (prawns prepared in fresh ginger with fresh red peppers and olive oil while on a layer of Basmati rice—and then throw in Bahji-style onion rings).

And those calories! The dessert menu is presented in a two-page leather folder and includes yet another nine categories: *cioccolato*, *fantasia*, *le café gourmand*, cookies, *cioccolatini*, special diets, *gelati*, *variegature*, and *sorbetti*. My cabin mate tried the *delizie al limone* (short crust dough, lemon cream, Italian meringue, and lemon caramel). Myself, it was the *vaniglia*: Tahitian vanilla bean ice cream on a collection of cubes of assorted fresh fruit.

Leaving the dining room: Jorge, the hugely charming, deeply elegant maître d' (from swank Cascais in Portugal) makes a point of asking: "And did you enjoy your dinner?"

After-dinner show: Very fine sextet of singers and all hosted by the very charming, very funny, and very unaffected Vickie van Tassel, cruise director (and—small world—is practically a neighbor, living in nearby in West New York, New Jersey).

The beautiful *Silver Whisper* moored at Fowey in Cornwall. (*Author's collection*)

Above left: Windstar Cruises introduced sail-cruise ships in 1986. (*Windstar Cruises*)

Above right: The Windstar vessels could also visit smaller, more remote ports. (*Windstar Cruises*)

Right: Windstar promoted a "country club casual" atmosphere onboard its ships. There was no formal dressing required. (*Windstar Cruises*)

27

A NEW BRAND: CRUISING WITH THE VIKINGS

She was docked in an unusual way for New York: stern first. But then she is an unusual ship. Unusual because she is so noticeably Scandinavian—like a fine Scandinavian hotel with Scandinavian decor, Scandinavian food (as one of many options), a reflection of Scandinavian living and well-being, and even a Scandinavian museum—and she is absolutely stunning—we might say Scandinavian stunning.

On an otherwise moody, cloud-filled October morning in 2016, the year-and-half-old *Viking Star* sailed along the Hudson River and put into Pier 88. The 47,800-ton ship (built in Italy by the ever-productive Fincantieri shipyards) is the first of six and later extended to eight and then fourteen identical sisters, all for the luxury market and all for Viking Ocean Cruises, the spinoff of hugely popular, fifty-five-river cruise ship-strong Viking River Cruises.

What a great treat to visit her on that overnight, maiden call to the Big Apple. The 748-foot-long *Viking Star* might just be the most instantly relaxing luxury cruise liners to come along in some time. The $700 million ship, designed by London- and Los Angeles-based decorators and designers, has been created to offer "soft elegance with a focus on destination—and discovery." The attention to detail, we found very quickly, is exceptional. The interiors, public space after public space, are intentionally "calmly and soothingly" color themed: almost all pale shades in blues, beiges, and light woods. In fact, the *Viking Star* is just about "glitz-free," and understated and uncluttered. You pick-up the tones quickly—puff and you feel more relaxed. In addition to the colors, there are lots of fine as well as eye-catching touches: localized lighting, cushions on chairs, even reindeer pelts on sofas.

We spent several hours onboard, and while we did not experience the likes of entertainment, restaurant dining, or ports of call, we found that—in quick view—the ship's five best features might be: overall decor; onboard mood and tone; the extreme friendliness and warmth of staff—and at every turn; the spa; and the absolute attention and high thinking to just about every last detail.

While her itineraries are generally port-intensive, the ship itself is like a destination in itself, like being in Scandinavia and in particular in Norway. There is Nordic artwork and photography throughout, vintage artifacts in glass cases, models of Viking ships, even little trolls peering as a backdrop to the elevator shafts. The upper-deck Wintergarden, for example, has latticed blonde wood branches that create a ceiling canopy and allow filtered daylight to "dance about" below. It might just feel like some Norwegian lodge.

Smiles! The staff is exceptional for its friendliness. We received a cheerful greeting at every turn, in every public area. Many of the staff are handpicked—coming from the likes of Seabourn, Cunard, and Crystal. One restaurant manager told us: "Viking takes superb care of its crew. They create happiness—and a very happy crew makes for happy care of the guests." Some 478 staff (from thirty-three countries) look after a maximum of 950 guests.

Down on Deck One, the spa, run by Sweden's Nordic LiV, is for starters luxuriously inviting. The space is so attractive as well:

Swedish limestone, black slate, juniper, and teak. It is also intended to be an "immersing experience," combining wellness with nature. There are pools, hot tubs, a steam room, and, of course, a sauna. Then there is the Snow Grotto. Sensibly balanced in temperatures, you can all but roll in the snow ("It's like being in a mini snow storm," added a spa manager from Stockholm) and then jump in the pool or the sauna or—with the pull of a cord—be rinsed by a bucket of chilled water. Up on deck, there is a midships pool covered by a retractable glass dome (and with some very cozily relaxing alcoves below) as well as a glass-backed infinity pool overlooking the stern. There is also a walk-around teak promenade and an outdoor gym area.

While we did not experience much in the way of dining (other than lunch), the *Viking Star* offers quite a lot, and, unusually, there is no extra charges for any of the specialty restaurants. The ship has in fact more al fresco seating than other cruise ship. Menus range from international, Italian-Mediterranean, regional, vegetarian, healthy living, and, of course, Scandinavian. Yes, it is all very diverse, very thoughtful, and very tempting. An Aquavit terrace, sushi bar, French patisserie, Italian gelateria, and—Mamsen's in the top-deck, splendid Explorers' Lounge—a Scandinavian counter offering fare such as open-faced roast beef sandwiches, fresh waffles, steak tartare on Norwegian rye bread, thick pea soup, and herring. Throughout the ship, wines are included at lunch and dinner and all while the *Viking Star* offers a very extensive beer collection.

The suites and staterooms are inviting, spacious, in a "space to spare" mode. All have verandas, generously sized closets, and big bathrooms capped with heated floors and walk-in showers. We visited one of the 370-square-foot junior suites highlighted with the likes of spacious living area, extra-long desk, and very fine bedding.

Viking Ocean Cruises is ambitious, innovative, and progressive. The *Viking Star* (following the wake of the superbly reputed Royal Viking Line of the 1970s and its top-rated ships *Royal Viking Star*, *Sea*, *Sky & Sun*) has been joined by the *Viking Sea*, the *Viking Sun* and, in 2019–20, the *Viking Spirit* and *Viking Song*. Viking offers a largely adults-only experience (sixteen is the minimum age for guests) as well as more enriching shore excursions and more overnights in ports of call than any other cruise line. Additionally, the Line offered its first world cruise in 2018 when the *Viking Sun* sets off on a very extensive 142-night itinerary (from Miami westabout to London) and, as reported by a staff member, "with lots and lots of overnights—including overnight in Havana."

Welcome to the "big ship" cruise business—Viking Ocean Cruises, we feel, will have a great future.

28

CRUISING EVOLUTION AND PROGRESS: 2013-17

In 2013, the North American cruise market was booming! Over 14 million passengers took cruises three years ago; by 2014, it reached over 17 million. Yet, almost ironically, only 20 percent of American vacationers have ever taken a cruise. Overall, worldwide cruise passengers amounted to less than half the annual visitors to Las Vegas. Obviously, there is a tremendously large untapped cruise market. The cruise lines see this. Alone in 2013, there were twenty-eight new cruise ships on order. By 2018, that number soared to 107 ships.

The mass-market cruise industry began to grow in serious numbers in the 1970s. Entire new companies with brand-new, purposely-built cruise ships came on line—companies such as Norwegian Cruise Lines, Royal Caribbean International, Princess Cruises and Carnival Cruise Lines. Americans began to see cruising as an ideal vacation and one with excellent value.

Furthermore, the cruise lines themselves made "friends" with their previous rival, the airlines, and created the very appealing air-sea vacation. Passengers could fly, say, from wintery, snowy New York and join a ship hours later at warm, tropical Miami and then head off on a sea-going vacation of three to fourteen days. Then there was the creation of theme cruises—on topics ranging from gardening to ballroom dancing, from investing to writing your own murder mystery—that appealed to passengers that might not otherwise sail. Third, there was the impact of the hugely popular television series *Love Boat*. It portrayed cruising in a fun, often younger light and each episode, seen by 35 million Americans each week, was said to generate as much as $10 million in positive advertising for cruising and the cruise lines themselves. Since 1970, when only 500,000 vacationers took cruises, there has been over 2,000 percent growth in American cruising.

Expansion continued, and almost beyond expectation, even imagination. Some forty new cruise ships debuted in the 1980s and then eighty new ships in the 1990s. Another 100 ships were added by the end of 2010. Carnival's rebuilt, 38,000-ton *Festivale* with 1,400 beds was the largest ship in Miami–Caribbean service in the late 1970s; today, it is the 227,000-ton *Harmony of the Seas*, carrying up to 6,600 passengers.

Six new cruise ships, including the likes of the 4,000-passenger *Norwegian Breakaway*, were added in 2013. Afterward, there were thirteen more new ships entering into service in 2014–15. New cruise lines were also emerging, such as Viking River Cruises, which is adding deep-sea operations (Viking Ocean Cruises) and with as many as four 50,000-ton, high-end, luxury cruise ships.

American passengers were then generally profiled at forty-six years of age with an annual income of $93,000. There had also been consistent growth in the family market—two adults and an average of two children. North American travelers came from every state in the U.S. and from throughout Canada. The states producing the most cruise passengers in the U.S. include the likes of California, New York, Florida, Arizona, New Jersey, and Texas.

American cruise lines had a 102 percent occupancy rate in 2012, and this despite the international recession and decline in spending on luxury items such as vacations. The primary reason has been

Above: Malaysian-owned Star Cruises has become a major cruise operator in the Far East. (*Star Cruises*)

Below: Spas have grown in size—and importance—on modern-day cruise liners. (*Cunard*)

Right: In a recent (2015) survey of vacationers who have never cruised, their highest aversion was to being tempted and offered too much food. (*Author's collection*)

Above left: Dance hosts are provided on many cruise lines. (*Author's collection*)

Above right: Disney's private island in the Bahamas. (*Disney Cruise Lines*)

Left: Disney entered cruising in 1998 and, expectedly, has been a great success. (*Disney Cruise Lines*)

Above: Disney has unique dining experiences and caters to a family trade as well. (*Disney Cruise Lines*)

Below: Port Everglades on a busy day. (*Port of Port Everglades Authority*)

Right: Cruise ships are built these days in Finland, Germany, France, and Italy, but in Finland and Germany, they are built in a huge sheds, like large garages. (*Author's collection*)

Above left: A Celebrity cruise ship is floated out—and soon to be fitted-out. (*Meyer Werft*)

Above right: Some eighty new cruise ships were building or in the planning by 2017. (*Wartsila Shipyard*)

discounting—and often massive discounting. Cruises have been offered from 50-percent reductions to as much as 75 percent. The offerings were so attractive and appealing that vacationers could do, for example, four nights to the Bahamas on the *Norwegian Jade* for $149, seven nights crossing the Atlantic on the *Queen Mary 2* for $499, and two weeks in the Mediterranean on the *Celebrity Eclipse* for $899. These offerings represent very appealing per diems of less than $100 per person per day. Internet sales have also allowed for many last-minute deals, filling ships just weeks before departure dates. "It becomes almost irresistible," said Michael Hadgis, who started cruising in 2007 and now has twelve voyages under his belt. "It is almost cheaper to cruise than to stay at home."

Cruise lines offset often deep discounting with the concept that passengers come aboard and then spend money during the voyage. Onboard spending includes the likes of casinos, gift shops, bars, shore excursions and photography. These create added income for the cruise lines. Overall, Americans spend the most while, as a comparison, Europeans spend far less while cruising.

Another appeal to cruising is itineraries. More and more, vacationers see cruising as the ideal way to travel, to see new lands and cities. It eliminates the likes of often costly hotels, finding restaurants, and creating entertainment. "The overall cruise concept is the ideal package of just about everything," added Margaret Webster. "You go can go ashore, say, after breakfast and do an all-day tour and then be back in time to the ship for a nap, drinks, dinner and a show. It is all perfect!"

The cruise lines are reaching out to more as well as diverse ports. Myself, in recent years, I visited Ghana and remote Principe Island off West Africa on a Crystal Cruises' ship; then, more recently, I visited off the beaten track Albania on a P&O cruise; and later cruised the

Norwegian fjords but in deep winter and for the chance to see the fabled Northern Lights.

Even the ships themselves are more appealing. They are more and more floating resorts, and they offer just about every amenity. There is cell phone access, Internet cafes, Wi-Fi Zones, rock climbing walls, zip lines, bowling alleys, surfing pools, shopping malls, sports bars, multi-room villas, multiple theme restaurants, and expansive spas. The *Oasis of the Seas* has an ice arena (for shows as well as passenger use) and an open-air diving arena.

Cruising can also be an alternative to flying. Many American travelers have grown unhappy with airlines, their reduced onboard services and increased costs (including those for baggage) as well as the airport processes (including long, sometimes delayed waits in security checkpoints). "Air travel, even for short distances, has become less and less appealing," said Scott Mitchell. "I try to avoid flying these days. Going by ship is much nicer and more appealing."

For North American cruise passengers, the Eastern Caribbean—including Puerto Rico, the Virgin Islands, and St. Maarten—remains the number one destination. The Western Caribbean—including Mexico, Jamaica and Grand Cayman—is second. Alaska is third, while the Mediterranean has become fourth. The busiest U.S. cruise embarkation ports are all in Florida and are Fort Lauderdale/Port Everglades in first place, then Miami and then Port Canaveral. Other U.S. ports are busy as well, such as New York, which sees 1 million cruise passengers per year. Interestingly, with the great growth in European cruising, Barcelona is currently the fourth busiest cruise port in the world.

On shore, in the U.S., the cruise industry generates nearly $36 billion a year in economic benefits, the cruise lines spend $17 billion a year in goods and shore-side services and altogether the cruise industry creates 314,000 landside jobs.

Overall, the Caribbean accounts for 34.4 percent of the entire world cruise market followed by 21.7 percent for the Mediterranean, 10.9 percent for Europe (excluding the Mediterranean), 5 percent for Australia and New Zealand, 4.8 percent for Alaska, 3.9 percent for South America, and 3.4 percent for Asia. Other, diverse cruise markets account for 15.8 percent.

Asia and Pacific cruise markets are seen as the next great areas of growth and especially for the largely untapped Chinese market. Since 2008, Australia cruising has increased by 155 percent and Asian cruising by 302 percent. Mega-cruise lines such as Carnival as well as Princess and Royal Caribbean are deploying ships to the Australian market while Royal Caribbean is assigning two large liners to regular cruising from Shanghai and Tianjin. Meanwhile, Princess is assigning two of its big liners to the Japanese market. Other markets are growing as well such as Brazil, which employed eighteen cruise liners last winter (the Brazilian summer). MSC Cruises offers voyages from South Africa as another example while Star Cruises has regular itineraries from Mumbai in India.

There are, of course, periodic shifts in cruise markets, such as political troubles in the Middle East and in Egypt, piracy off East Africa, downturns in European economies (such as Greece and Spain), and even the tragic, headline-making sinking of the *Costa Concordia* in January 2012. Shortly thereafter, the much-publicized breakdown of the *Carnival Triumph* sent some negative ripples through the industry as well.

New ships will continue to add more amenities—be more exciting, more appealing. The 144,000-ton *Norwegian Breakaway*, for example, will offer a cupcake shop and dance classes by members of New York City's famed Rockettes, while the 167,000-ton *Quantum of the Seas*, commissioned in fall 2014, offered virtual balconies for inside cabins as well as a circus school and a showroom complete with bumper cars. "Cruising is very addictive. I've done fifty cruises in the past fifteen years," said Richard Goldman. "It is the most wonderful vacation. I hope to do fifty more cruises!"

A year later, in 2014, a friend had just returned from a mid-winter, seven-night cruise from New York south to the sun—to the Bahamas and Florida—aboard the year-old *Norwegian Breakaway*. It was her fourth trip on that 4,000-passenger ship in the past six months. "I love the escape, the relaxation, just being aboard the ship," she told me. "I am not interested in the ports, but the shipboard experience—the food, the spa and the wonderful service." She traveled in the 145,000-ton liner's exclusive, upper Haven Class, reserved for a mere 200 or so guests. It all very private, well served, and highly pampered. On her most recent *Breakaway* cruise, however, she sailed off with a 75 percent discount, lowering the normally $3,000 fare to $1,400. "We just could not resist," she added.

While the cruise industry worldwide is busy, very popular, and expanding (with nearly two dozen more cruise ships coming on line), discounting in these financially tight times is very common

Above: Modern-day cruise ships are indeed floating cities—and floating resorts. (*Princess Cruises*)

Below left: Ships carrying 4,000 and 5,000 passengers have become almost common place by 2015. (*Royal Caribbean Cruise Lines*)

Below right: Norwegian Cruise Lines' 2,750-passenger *Norwegian Gem* departing from New York's Pier 88. (*Author's collection*)

Above left: Future cruising! (*Wartsila Shipyard*)

Above right: Ideas for giant vessels. (*Author's collection*)

Below left: High-speed cruise ships. (*Author's collection*)

Below right: Indeed, like floating islands. (*Author's collection*)

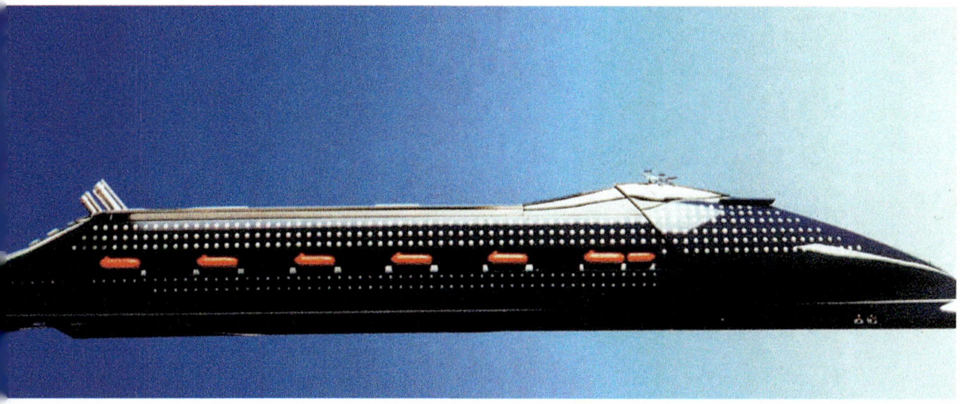

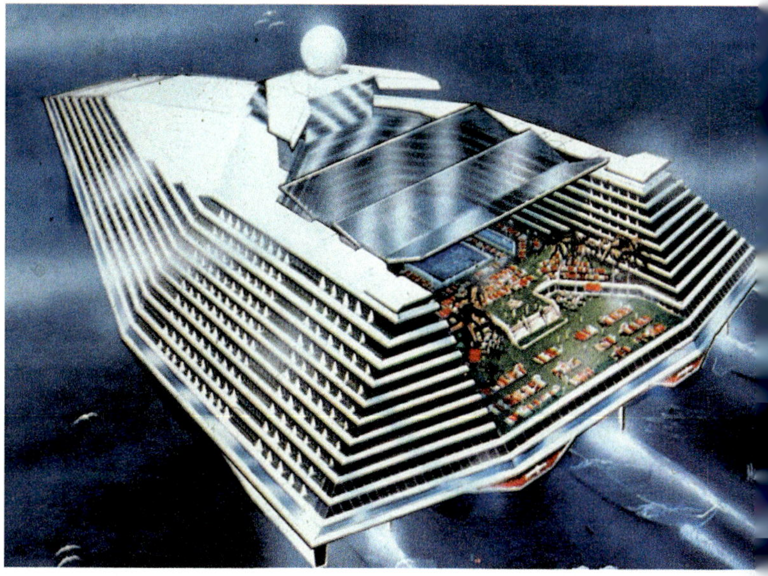

(cruise lines compensate with onboard spending: tours, bars, photo shop, etc.). It often fills the ships—and to the very last cabin. Some of the latest offerings in the American cruise market, the biggest in the world, include eye-opening reductions such as $149 for four days to the Bahamas, $399 for a week in the Caribbean, and $699 for twelve nights in the Mediterranean. A weeklong crossing between New York and Southampton aboard the legendary *Queen Mary 2* was offered recently for $799 (or slightly more than $100 per person per day).

Numbers are impressive—discounting or not! Demand is high. Last Christmas–New Year, I was aboard the superb *Crystal Serenity* for her two-week holiday cruise. Every cabin was booked and, at the last minute, Crystal staff were scrambling to find extra berths. In February, while aboard Cunard's *Queen Elizabeth*, a high number of nearly 400 passengers were taking the complete 120-day World Cruise. There were 800 taking the *Queen Mary*'s ninety-five-day World Cruise and 500 are already booked on next year's World voyage aboard the *Crystal Serenity*. In the short cruise market, the *Explorer of the Seas* departed from New York in mid-February with a record high of 3,800 passengers aboard (and this was out of 3,600 lower berths). Royal Caribbean as well as Princess have reported record high numbers on some voyages as well. Quite simply, and especially with discounts from 50–75 percent, cruising is seen as excellent value. To many, it is the perfect, very affordable vacation.

With over 200 cruise ships already in service, there are over 100 coming on late by 2018 and beyond. The biggest will be two or possibly three more of the *Oasis of the Seas* class, 225,000-plus tonners that can carry up to 6,600 passengers and 2,800 crew. Costing close to $2 billion each to build, these Royal Caribbean mega-liners will be the biggest passenger ships ever created—six times the size of the *Titanic* of 1912 and three times the size of the original *Queen Mary* of 1936. And there are others—Royal Caribbean was adding twin 167,000 tonners of his innovative *Quantum* class, Germany's TUI Cruises was constructing a pair of 100,000-ton liners for their largely German clientele, P&O was adding the 141,000-ton *Britannia* for the U.K. cruise trade and, as a new comer to the high-end, luxury market, there were no less than four 47,000-ton ships being created for the six-star Viking Ocean Cruises. There was still more, including the possibility of a 56,000-ton, 2,345-passenger recreation of the immortal *Titanic* for Australian-financed Blue Star Cruises.

Almost all major cruise lines have not only increased in size, but offer bigger ships with bigger capacities. Holland America Line, as an example, had three cruise liners thirty years ago; today, they have fifteen ships and added their biggest yet, a 99,000-tonner, in 2016. For years, Cunard had either one or two Queens, but now they have three. Britain's P&O Cruises has seven ships and Italy's Costa with fourteen. Miami-based Carnival Corporation is all-time "winner and champ"—they own a dozen cruise lines, which altogether have 105 liners and jointly control just under 50 percent of the world's cruise market, touching at ports from Bermuda to Brisbane, from Bergen to Buenos Aires.

The biggest and therefore most profitable cruise market is North American (the U.S. and Canada) with an estimated 17 million annual cruise passengers this year (and growing upwards to 22 million in five years). This is followed by the British and German cruise markets with some 2 million each per year. Other countries are showing increases as well. Recently, there has been significant growth in the Brazilian cruise market, but very high growth in the Australian cruise business (up by 155 percent in the last five years). "More and more Australians are seeing cruising as a wonderful vacation," said a passenger from Melbourne. "We even fly overseas, say to Rome or London or San Francisco, just to take a cruise!" The biggest growth in the immediate future, however, and according to almost all industry pundits, will be in Asia. The Japanese, South Korean, Southeast Asian, but most especially the Chinese markets will climb upward significantly, even soar. Asian cruising has increased by a staggering 300 percent in the past five years. Carnival, Royal Caribbean, Princess, and Malaysian-based Star Cruises are among those adding bigger and bigger ships with Far Eastern-based itineraries.

Other areas are also booming: the Mediterranean is now the second most popular cruising destination (with a 22 percent place amid the world market), seeing the huge, 6,400-passenger *Allure of the Seas* based in Barcelona in 2015. European river boat cruising is also soaring. Alone, Viking River Cruises has added some three-dozen brand-new river cruisers.

The future is not just bright, but very bright. "There's nothing like a cruise. It is the best vacation of all," said New Yorker Marjorie Wells. "I've done fifty cruises in the past twenty-five years and plan to do at least fifty more in the next twenty-five years!!

By 2015, the cruise business continued to boom! Near to the end of the year, no less than thirty-four cruise ships were being built—or at least firmly in the planning stages or on order. That is a record! European shipyards, specialists in cruise liner construction, in Italy, France, Germany, Finland, and Japan are all but crammed—fully booked with billions of dollars' worth of construction.

Six liners were added to worldwide cruising in 2015, nine joined in 2016, six in 2017, and eight were due in 2018. Alone, the mighty Carnival Corporation has at least two-dozen new liners on order and these are to be divided among several of its subsidiary lines. Cruising numbers have been steadily increasing: from 19 million five years ago, in 2010, to 23 million this year. It is expected to exceed 25 million by 2020. In a recent survey of 100,000 American vacationers, 42 percent voted that a cruise was the very best overall vacation against 14 percent citing a land-based vacation and 9 percent for a resort vacation.

The typical cruise passenger in the U.S. is forty-nine years old, married, has a college education, and earns an average of $114,000 a year.

Three to seven-day cruises are the most popular, appealing to families of two adults and two children. Some 62 percent of all American cruise passengers are returning customers. In a similar survey, the top three benefits of a cruise were cited: 70 percent select a cruise because it is the very best way to see several locations; 60 percent cited the rest, relaxation, and "get away" qualities offered by a cruise; and another 60 percent named the pampering during a cruise as a top benefit. Carnival Corporation—with some 105 ships and over a dozen subsidiaries—generated the highest income in 2014 with nearly $16 billion. Royal Caribbean and its subsidiaries followed at $8 billion. Norwegian Cruise Lines did $3 billion, followed by MSC with $1.5 billion, Disney $950 million, Thomson $700 million, and Asia's Star Cruises just a tad under Thomson.

The list of new builds is all but mind-boggling. Royal Caribbean leads the list with no less than two 227,000-ton liners under construction. Slightly larger versions of the highly successful *Oasis of the Seas* and *Allure of the Seas*, the first of these 1,188-foot long mega-liners, to be named *Harmony of the Seas* and building at St. Nazaire in France, will be delivered in 2016. Costing $1.5 billion, it will be the biggest passenger ship of all time and will carry a maximum of 6,360 passengers. Meanwhile, though not quite as large, several new Carnival ships will carry up to 6,600 passengers—the highest cruise capacities yet. Also under construction, Aida has at least four new liners coming into service: a pair of 183,000-tonners and another pair of 124,000 ton ships. Costa will add it biggest liners yet, a pair of 183,000 ton liners, while Royal Caribbean is planning for two more *Quantum of the Seas* class 4,900-bed ships. Both MSC and Norwegian Cruise Lines each have four liners on liner while Star Cruises and Celebrity each have ordered pairs of new vessels. A new entrant is Virgin Cruises, beginning with a trio of 110,000 tonners, carrying 2,800 passengers each. Perhaps the greatest expansion for 2015 was Crystal Cruises, a part of Genting Hong Kong from last May. Crystal had what might have been the biggest cruise news ever. Crystal revealed an almost startling four-prong plan: three 100,000-ton cruise liners for 1,000 passengers, with 1,000 crew and with a top deck for suites that guests can buy; Crystal yacht/expedition cruise using two sixty-two-bed luxury ships; Crystal luxury river cruises in Europe; and around-the-world luxury tours in a luxurious Crystal jet.

Other notations included the opening of the Cuban cruise market and with the likes of Carnival and MSC quickly making itinerary plans. Historically, Cunard turned 175, Princess had its fiftieth anniversary and Crystal its twenty-fifth.

Specialist cruising is thriving as are riverboat voyages, especially in Europe. Food/cooking and wine theme cruises remain the most popular. Wellness, fitness, history, poker and even motorcycle cruises are increasing in popularity. More specifically, family reunion cruises are also on the rise.

Surveyed passengers reported preferences in selecting a cruise. A cruise providing an experience to remember had the highest score followed by the ability to stay connected during a voyage. Third was the ability to travel in groups followed by the service provided by staff and crew and, finally, the food.

Ten years ago, passengers selected ship by its reputation as the primary reason for selecting a particular voyage. Five years ago, this changed to itinerary. In 2015, it was price, followed by itinerary, and, in last place, reputation of the ship.

A total of 36 percent of American cruise passengers selected the Caribbean as their favorite destination followed by 20 percent for the Mediterranean, 11 percent for Northern Europe, and 6 percent for Australia, New Zealand, and the South Pacific. China is growing in vast numbers. It is expected to become the second largest worldwide cruise market and, perhaps by 2025, surpass the biggest of all, the 18 million cruisers in the U.S. The growth of the Chinese markets includes plans to begin building passenger liners in specially prepared Chinese shipyards. At least a half dozen Chinese cruise lines have sprung up recently, and with high interest from established cruise operators, China cruising might be equated to a convoy. Princess Cruises, for example, has assigned the 2,675-passenger *Sapphire Princess* to year-round Chinese cruise service. Meanwhile, Royal Caribbean is way ahead in China cruising there with four and soon to be five giant liners. The 4,180-bed *Quantum of the Seas* has joined fleet mates *Voyager of the Seas*, *Mariner of the Seas*, and *Legend of the Seas*. They will be joined by another 4,180-berth ship, the upcoming *Ovation of the Seas*. Costa is second runner-up with four big liners in Chinese cruise service: *Costa Fortuna*, *Costa Serena*, *Costa Atlantica*, and *Costa Victoria*.

Among the top ten busiest cruise ports for 2015, Miami has the slight edge over nearby Port Everglades. Port Canaveral, also in Florida, was third busiest followed by Nassau, Cozumel, Barcelona, Civitavecchia (for Rome), St. Thomas, St. Maarten, and Venice. Barcelona is now the busiest cruise port in Europe.

Sun-drenched ports and luncheon buffets on deck, Broadway shows and robotic bartenders, rock climbing walls and bumper cars—cruising and cruise ships are expanding like never before!

Yes, 2016 was another very busy year: the total number of worldwide cruise passengers jumped up, seven new cruise liners were introduced (including the largest passenger liner ever), and some fifty other ships are building, on order (and later increased to over eighty) or in the drawing stages well into the 2020s. Honestly, I cannot quite keep track of it all, of all the ships and which goes with which, but business is booming, and cruise ships seem to be getting bigger and bigger—200,000 tons and 5,000 passengers seem no longer to raise eyebrows. Also, these ships are ordered in pairs, but more often in groups. Added news is that each of these new ships seem to have a special amenity, an added selling point, a hook. Trends seem to be less glitzy decor, fewer big showrooms, and more dining options. More specifically, it was the year of simpler colors, funky little dining options, and the likes of an IMAX theater and an elevated bicycle course. Once again (and based on a recent survey), there will be far less regimentation—eat when and where you want, for example. There will also be more intimate entertainment venues, and in stateroom technology, environmentally friendly power systems, and—thank all the sea gods—faster internet.

A few facts: 24 million travelers took cruises in 2016, from overnight gambling junkets from Hong Kong and Singapore to four months around the world on each of Cunard's *Queens*. The Caribbean remained the number one destination by far, attracting 34 percent of all passengers, and was followed by the Mediterranean with nearly 19 percent. There was a total 475 cruise options last year, from 6,600-bed super mega ships to freighters carrying six passengers. River cruising, especially in Europe, showed great growth and added no fewer than eighteen new vessels. Germany grew, China is exploding, and the Australian cruise market jumped from 158,000 cruisers in 2004 to 1.2 million twelve years later.

Highpoint among the new 2016 ships was the 227,700-ton *Harmony of the Seas*, the biggest passenger ship of all time. At Civitavecchia (the port for Rome), we berthed there last June when the *Harmony* arrived. We were on Cunard's 92,000-ton *Queen Elizabeth*, but altogether seemed overwhelmed, outdone, even humbled. Costing $1½ billion to construct (in France), the 1,187-foot-long *Harmony* is a slightly enhanced, slightly bigger version of the 225,282-ton *Oasis of the Seas* and her twin, the *Allure of the Seas*. The *Harmony* is huge, towering, and mighty, and she is true Royal Caribbean: her amenities among her seventeen decks include an aqua theater with divers, a bionic bar where drinks are served by robots, the musical *Grease*, a Central Park open court, a carousel, and a water park highlighted by the Ultimate Abyss, the tallest slide yet to go to sea. Families love the *Harmony*, but then so do eighty-year-old grandmothers!

Meanwhile, Carnival Cruise Lines is stepping-up their game, and getting-up more steam in competing with innovative Royal Caribbean and even the-getting-bigger-by-the-day Norwegian Cruise Lines. Carnival's new 3,934-bed *Carnival Horizon* was the largest Carnival ship yet and has a long list of amenities: that IMAX theatre; an onboard brewery (and serving three house-made beers); an open-air cycling ride (an 800-ft long track is suspended above the ship's top deck); staterooms with a Cuban theme; a sky ropes course; a 3-D Thrill Theatre; and even a family-focused "hangout" club.

Viking Cruises—in the wake of creating the largest river boat fleet—added its second liner, the 48,000-grt, 928-berth *Viking Sea*. Mirroring the old Royal Viking Line and its celebrated standards and style, several sisters will follow. The *Sea* is indeed stunning and is highlighted by her Scandinavian decorative style; the "Spa & Snow" Grotto; and an inclusive fare that includes (thank you!) the likes of internet, specialty restaurants, wines, and one shore excursion in every port.

On the high luxury side, Regent added the 738-passenger *Silver Seas Explorer*, which they have dubbed "the most luxurious ship at sea." Supporting that is a 3,900-square foot, two-bedroom suite complete with private spa, which sells for $10,000 per day. Note: shore excursions are included in the fare for everyone. Similarly, Seabourn added their largest luxurious vessel, the 600-passenger *Seabourn Encore.* Very, very sleek on the inside; having the popular Seabourn Square; and a veranda for every suite.

Holland America added its biggest liner yet as well, the 99,000-ton *Koningsdam*. She features a Music Walk; B. B. King Blues Club; a Lincoln Center Stage; and family suites for up to five.

The year 2016 had other notations: the "remastering" of the eleven-year-old *Queen Mary 2*; developing plans for Virgin Cruise Lines; more new ships for the Chinese market; increased deployment of ships to Australia; the struggling Eastern Mediterranean and Mid-Eastern markets; the opening of Cuba; the failure of Carnival's Fathom cruise operation; the collapse of British niche cruise line Voyages of Discovery; and much more!

Interesting to see, by the end of 2016, the list of the world's largest passenger ships and who owns what:

Name of ship	Owner	Weight	Length
Harmony of the Seas	RCI	226,963 grt	1,188 feet
Allure of the Seas	RCI	225,282 grt	1,187 feet
Oasis of the Seas	RCI	225,283 grt	1,187 feet
Quantum of the Seas	RCI	168,666 grt	1,139 feet
Anthem of the Seas	RCI	168,666 grt	1,139 feet
Ovation of the Seas	RCI	168,666 grt	1,142 feet
Norwegian Escape	NCL	165,167 grt	1,069 feet
Liberty of the Seas	RCI	155,889 grt	1,112 feet
Norwegian Epic	NCL	155,873 grt	1,081 feet
Freedom of the Seas	RCI	154,407 grt	1,112 feet
Independence of the Seas	RCI	154,407 grt	1,112 feet
Genting Dream	Dream	150,698 grt	1,100 feet
Queen Mary 2	Cunard	149,215 grt	1,132 feet

But no matter the ship or the voyage, there is nothing quite like a cruise! (*Holland-America Line*)

BIBLIOGRAPHY

Fiebig, R., Heine, F., and Lose, F., *Great Passenger Ships of the World* (Hamburg: Koehlers Publishing Co., 2015)

Haws, D., *Merchant Fleets: Holland America Line* (Uckfield, England: TCL Publications, 1995)

Heine, F., and Lose, F., *Great Passenger Ships of the World* (Hamburg: Koehlers Publishing Co., 2010)

Kludas, A., *Great Passenger Ships of the World* (Volumes 1–5); *Great Passenger Ships of the World* (Wellingborough, Northamptonshire: Patrick Stephens Ltd., 1984 and 1992); *Great Passenger Ships of the World* (Hamburg: Koehlers Publishing Co., 1987, 1997)

Kludas, A., Heine, F., and Lose, F., *Great Passenger Ships of the World* (Hamburg: Koehlers Publishing Co., 2002, 2006)

Mayes, W., *Cruise Ships* (5th edition) (Windsor, England: Oceanview Press Ltd., 2015)

Official Steamship Guide (New York City: Transportation Guides Inc., 1953–63)